a strongly
held on strongly
affirmed
aesp a a tion,
oes a ction,
gu a a
guadell e on or
achievement

CREDO

KNOW YOUR STORY

CONFIRM YOUR FAITH

LIVE YOUR COMMITMENT

Confirmation Teaching Plans
for 8 Weeks

CREDO

a strongly held or strongly affirmed ... conviction, ... a creed ... emotion or

WRITERS

Tim Gossett

Kevin Alton

Rev. Dee Dee Azhikakath

Rev. Karen Kluever

Kara Lassen Oliver

Mark Ray

Rev. Chris Hughes

Rev. Taylor Burton-Edwards

Lanecia Rouse

EDITORIAL AND DESIGN TEAM

Josh Tinley — Development Editor

Sheila K. Hewitt — Production Editing Supervisor

Keely Moore — Design Manager

ADMINISTRATIVE STAFF

Neil M. Alexander — Publisher

Marjorie M. Pon — Editor, Church School Publications

CREDO CONFIRMATION TEACHING PLANS FOR 8 WEEKS: An official resource for The United Methodist Church, approved by the General Board of Discipleship and published by Cokesbury, The United Methodist Publishing House, 201 Eighth Avenue, South, P.O. Box 801, Nashville, TN 37202-0801. Copyright © 2011 by Cokesbury.

To order copies of this publication, call toll-free 800-672-1789. Call Monday through Friday, 7:00–6:30 Central Time; 5:00–4:30 Pacific Time; Saturday, 9:00–5:00. You may fax your order to 800-445-8189. Telecommunication Device for the Deaf/Telex Telephone: 800-227-4091. Use your Cokesbury account, American Express, Visa, Discover, or MasterCard.

Scripture quotations in this publication, unless otherwise indicated, are from the *New Revised Standard Version of the Bible,* copyright © 1989 by the Division of Christian Education of the National Council of the Churches of Christ in the United States of America, and are used by permission. All rights reserved.

12 13 14 15 16 17 18 19 20 — 10 9 8 7 6 5 4 3 2

Contents

CREDO Contributors

KEVIN ALTON is a United Methodist youth worker, worship leader, writer, husband, father, and friend. In his free time, Kevin enjoys songwriting and recording with his band, Purrington. Kevin has a passion for confirmation and being present as youth take these steps along their spiritual journey. Kevin lives near Chattanooga with his wife, Britta, and their two boys, Grey and Penner.

REV. DEE DEE AZHIKAKATH is an ordained elder in the Desert Southwest Annual Conference and has experience working in churches in Texas, New Jersey, Arizona, and England. She has served on the General Commission on Religion and Race and the General Board of Church and Society and has taught confirmation in rural, multi-church settings; in large, suburban churches; and in campus ministry.

TIM GOSSETT is a long-time youth ministry and Christian education veteran, having worked as a youth director, a campus ministry assistant, a Christian education director, a writer, an editor, and a member of a camp staff. A graduate of United Theological Seminary, with degrees in Religious Education and Religious Communications, he is the author of several youth ministry books. He lives in Ames, Iowa, with his wife and son.

REV. KAREN TROGDON KLUEVER is a deacon in the South Carolina Conference, serves as a minister to youth and college students, and has more than 20 years of youth ministry experience. She developed *Synago*, a student-led, small-group Bible study, and has designed models for confirmation and Bible study in her local church. Karen has a master's in Christian education from Pfeiffer University. She lives in Charlotte, North Carolina.

KARA LASSEN OLIVER, while at Vanderbilt Divinity School, took a job at the United Methodist National Youth Ministry Organization (now the Division on Ministries With Young People). She later moved into full-time youth ministry in a local church in Nashville, Tennessee, and became a writer and editor. She wrote for CREDO while serving with her family as Volunteers in Mission in Malawi.

MARK RAY, in more than 15 years as a volunteer at Christ Church United Methodist in Louisville, Kentucky, has taught middle school and high school Sunday school, led confirmation, and slept on more hard floors and smelly mattresses than he cares to remember. He has authored or contributed to several curriculum and programming resources.

REV. CHRIS HUGHES is a writer, musician, retreat leader, and United Methodist pastor in Salisbury, North Carolina. For several years, Chris and his wife, Gloria, have led confirmation retreats for the Southeastern Jurisdiction of The United Methodist Church. Chris has written and recorded music for several worship resources.

REV. TAYLOR BURTON-EDWARDS is an ordained elder, serving as Director of Worship Resources with the General Board of Discipleship. He received his Master of Divinity from The Southern Baptist Theological Seminary and his M.A. from Associated Mennonite Biblical Seminary. Taylor and his wife, Grace, have two sons, Jacob and Will.

LANECIA ROUSE is the project manager for the Art Project of Houston, a homeless ministry affiliated with St. John's Downtown United Methodist Church. A graduate of Duke Divinity School, she spent more than six years as a youth pastor in Nashville, Tennessee, and Leeds, England.

Review Team

SARAH ARTHUR
Youth Ministry Author and Speaker
Lansing, Michigan

REV. STEPHEN CADY
United Methodist Pastor
Kansas East Annual Conference

BISHOP MINERVA CARCAÑO
United Methodist Bishop
Desert Southwest Annual Conference

REV. TERRY CARTY
Executive Director, Youth Worker
   Movement
United Methodist Pastor
Tennessee Annual Conference

KIM GEORGE
United Methodist Children's Director
Arlington, Texas

REV. JENNY HALLENBECK
United Methodist Pastor
Dakotas Annual Conference

REV. SUSAN HAY
Director, Youth Ministries
General Board of Discipleship

BISHOP ROBERT HOSHIBATA
United Methodist Bishop
Oregon Idaho Annual Conference

DR. SONDRA MATTHAEI
United Methodist Professor
   of Christian Religious Education
St. Paul School of Theology,
Kansas City, Missouri

DR. M. DOUGLAS MEEKS
Professor and Chair in Wesleyan
   Studies and Theology
Vanderbilt Divinity School,
Nashville, Tennessee

BLAIR GILMER MEEKS
United Methodist Author and Liturgy
   Specialist
Nashville, Tennessee

ERICA MUNOZ
Children, Youth, and Young Adult
   Coordinator
Greater New Jersey Annual Conference

REV. MIKE RATLIFF
Associate General Secretary, Division
   on Ministries With Young People
General Board of Discipleship

REV. BRYAN TENER
United Methodist Pastor
Oklahoma Annual Conference

DR. ED TRIMMER
Chair, Department of Religion
Professor of Youth Ministry
Huntingdon College,
Montgomery, Alabama

DEVELOPMENT TEAM AND CONSULTANTS

DEVELOPMENT TEAM

Neal Bowes

Stephanie Hand

Chris Hughes

Karen Kluever

Camille Mattick

J.C. Mitchell

Shelly Petz

CONSULTANTS

Sarah Arthur

Ann Cover

Timothy Eberhart

Jacob Fasig

Susan Hay

MaryJane Pierce Norton

Introduction and Core Principles

Before you do anything else, grab a copy of *The United Methodist Hymnal* and turn to page 33. Read the "Baptismal Covenant I," a service that many United Methodist congregations use to confirm young people who have completed the church's confirmation program. The service begins by describing confirmation as a "reaffirmation of our faith," a renewal of "the covenant declared at our baptism," an acknowledgment of "what God is doing for us," and an affirmation of "our commitment to Christ's holy church."

This statement gives a good overview of the goals of any confirmation program. Confirmation is an opportunity for young people to affirm the faith into which they were baptized and, for those who were baptized as infants or small children, to renew the baptismal vows taken for them by their parents or guardians. Confirmation also makes young people aware of how God is and has been at work in their lives, even before they were old enough to realize it. And confirmation affirms a new commitment—a new covenant relationship—between a young person and Christ's body, the church.

CORE PRINCIPLES

The CREDO (CREE-doh) confirmation program is grounded in these three core principles:

> ❥ Confirmation is the continuation of one's faith journey (a journey begun at baptism) and the beginning of one's covenant relationship with the church—not an end unto itself.

> ❥ Confirmation is more than just a series of classes. Confirmands must be fully engaged in the life of the church through worship, service, small groups, and involvement in other ministries.

> ❥ Confirmands should emerge from their confirmation experience prepared for a life of Christian discipleship.

CREDO reinforces the connection between baptism and confirmation. Confirmands will remember their baptism (or, if they have not yet been baptized, anticipate their baptism) and learn about the baptismal vows that they took, that they will take, or that were taken on their behalf. Confirmands will understand confirmation as a way to claim and affirm the work done by the Holy Spirit in their baptism.

EMPHASES

Instruction is an important and essential part of any confirmation program. Through confirmation, young people claim the faith of the church. They must have a familiarity with what Christians (and specifically United Methodist

Christians) believe, value, and do. Thus Credo provides session plans for confirmation classes. But instruction is only one aspect of the confirmation program. The confirmation vows not only hold confirmands accountable to certain beliefs but are also a way of life and a commitment to Christ's body, the church. In addition to learning about their faith, confirmands must also experience their faith and have a sense of how to live as a disciple of Christ in a covenant relationship with the church. They do this by attending and participating in weekly Sunday worship, by working alongside other Christians in service of God and neighbor, by participating in Christian education, by having relationships with other Christians that are grounded in mutual support and accountability, and by being engaged in the ministries of the church.

Christian Education

Your confirmation program is an important Christian education ministry, but it is not likely the only education opportunity for young people. And it is impossible (yes, impossible) for a confirmand to learn everything he or she needs to know about the Bible, Christian faith, and Christian living before confirmation Sunday. Christian education is a lifelong endeavor, and young people should make Christian education a habit by participating in educational opportunities such as Sunday school classes, mid-week Bible study groups, and/or youth fellowship gatherings. If it is possible, your confirmands should be involved in at least one other Christian education setting while they are going through the confirmation program.

Mentoring Relationships

Mentors should be adults with a mature faith who can set for young confirmands an example of how to grow in faith. Confirmands and their mentors should meet regularly for the duration of the confirmation program. Mentors are not teachers and need not be Bible experts or trained theologians. But they should be available to offer support and encouragement, to talk with confirmands about tough faith questions, and to discuss with confirmands the key teachings of the confirmation program. More comprehensive information on mentoring is available in the "Mentoring and Confirmation" section of this resource and in the book *Credo Confirmation Guide for Parents, Mentors, and Adult Leaders*.

Worship

Often when people talk about "going to church," they are talking about attending worship. While *worship* and *church* are not synonymous, worship is crucial to the life of the church and of each individual congregation. Worship is a way that we tell our story and pass down our beliefs and practices to subsequent generations; it is a way that Christians of all "ages, nations, and races" come together to express their common faith; and it is a way that we say yes to the God who said yes to us through our baptism. Being present each week in worship is an important way in which young people honor the commitment to the church, a commitment they make when they take their confirmation vows. It is important that young people get into the habit of attending worship while they are going through the confirmation program so that they will understand what is expected of them if they take the confirmation vows.

service

Although he was the Son of God and the Messiah, Jesus became a servant (see **Philippians 2:7**). He served others by healing, feeding, and teaching and by washing his disciples' feet. Following Jesus' example of service always has been an important part of Christian discipleship, and those who take the confirmation vows in The United Methodist Church vow to "faithfully participate in [the church's] ministries" by (among other things) their service. While the word *service* may bring to mind images of raking leaves or restoring homes (and while these activities are important), service is about more than just work projects. Young people in the church may serve as acolytes, ushers, or greeters during worship; they may serve God and neighbor by raising money for missions and ministries that meet needs in the community and around the world; they may serve members of the congregation by praying and worshiping with persons who are physically unable to attend Sunday worship; they may serve by helping to lead a vacation Bible school program for younger children; and they may get their hands dirty by participating in the aforementioned work projects. Confirmands must understand that service is an important part of Christian living, that those who are confirmed in The United Methodist Church take a vow of service, and that the service must be performed in a spirit of love for God and neighbor. To get in the habit of serving, confirmands should be expected to complete a certain number of service hours as part of the confirmation program.

retreats

The word *retreat* means to get away or to withdraw. And while retreats give us opportunities to withdraw from our normal routine, they also give us an opportunity to draw closer to God and to our fellow Christians. On retreats, young Christians can experience God and Christian community without the distractions of television, mobile phones, the Internet, schoolwork, and household obligations. CREDO recommends that every confirmand participate in at least one retreat.

sessions

Although CREDO emphasizes that confirmation is more than just a series of classes, confirmation class sessions are nonetheless a critical part of the confirmation experience. These sessions tell confirmands the story of our faith, teach them about core Christian beliefs and practices, explain to them distinct United Methodist emphases, and help them develop a faith vocabulary. They fall into three units: "Know Your Story," "Confirm Your Faith," and "Live Your Commitment."

CREDO Goals

The underlying goals of CREDO are to prepare confirmands (if they choose) to take the confirmation vows and to live lives of Christian discipleship. More specifically, CREDO aims to:

➤ Teach confirmands the story of their faith, as contained in the Old and New Testaments and in the history and traditions of Christianity and The United Methodist Church.

➤ Give confirmands a basic understanding of Christian theology, including the doctrine of the Trinity, creation, sin, and grace.

➤ Teach confirmands the traditions and doctrinal emphases that make United Methodism unique.

➤ Foster relationships between confirmands and Christian adults in the congregation who can set an example of how to live as a mature Christian.

➤ Give confirmands an understanding of the importance of Christian education as a lifelong endeavor, and help confirmands develop a habit of participating in Christian education.

➤ Give confirmands an understanding of Christian worship as practiced in The United Methodist Church and why worship is an essential part of Christian discipleship.

➤ Challenge confirmands to serve God and others through the life and ministry of the congregation.

➤ Give confirmands an opportunity to go on retreats, withdrawing from their normal routine and drawing closer to God and their fellow Christians.

➤ Teach confirmands about the vows they will have an opportunity to take and the commitments that one makes when one says yes to those vows.

CREDO Components

In addition to this book, CREDO offers the following print and electronic resources to help you achieve for your small church the goals listed on page 11:

CREDO CONFIRMATION STUDENT JOURNAL

The *CREDO Confirmation Student Journal* is not a traditional classroom student book. Instead of providing confirmands pen-and-paper activities to complete in the classroom, it encourages them to develop habits of prayer and devotion. The Student Journal includes a devotional reading and journaling questions related to each confirmation class session. In the days following each class session, confirmands should read that session's devotion and spend time reflecting on and/or writing in response to the journaling questions. Confirmands also should discuss their reflections and writings with their confirmation mentor.

The CREDO CONFIRMATION STUDENT JOURNAL also challenges confirmands to write a credo, or statement of belief, as they go through the confirmation program. After each session, they will complete a sentence that summarizes their belief about what they learned in that session. Taken together, these sentences will be a written affirmation of the confirmands' faith.

CREDO CONFIRMATION GUIDE FOR PARENTS, MENTORS, AND ADULT LEADERS

Confirmation is not just a personal rite. It involves the families of the confirmands and the entire congregation. For many Christians faith formation begins at home. And while the congregation strives to nurture young Christians in the faith, parents and/or guardians provide many of these fledgling disciples day-to-day support. But parents are by no means alone in this effort. Each confirmand should have a confirmation mentor, an adult in the congregation with whom he or she will meet regularly throughout the confirmation process (and possibly beyond). Other adults in the congregation who work with confirmands, such as youth and children's ministers, Sunday school teachers, and music ministers, also play important roles in the confirmands' faith development. And, of course, as those being confirmed stand before the congregation on Confirmation Sunday, the entire congregation vows to "Do all in [its] power to increase *their* faith, confirm *their* hope, and perfect *them* in love" (*The United Methodist Hymnal*, page 43).

The *Credo Confirmation Guide for Parents, Mentors, and Adult Leaders* gives these adults information about what confirmands are learning and experiencing in their confirmation classes so that they can have meaningful conversations about topics such as grace and redemption and the Wesleyan quadrilateral. The book also provides valuable information about adolescent development as it relates to faith formation.

CREDO CONFIRMATION MULTIMEDIA TEACHING TOOLS

CREDO Confirmation Multimedia Teaching Tools includes a DVD with 18 original videos that introduce topics such as sin, redemption, the church, worship, sacraments, and grace, and review the confirmation vows. (This book includes instructions on using the video with your confirmation classes.) *Multimedia Teaching Tools* also includes a CD loaded with PowerPoint slide shows, high-resolution graphics, and printable posters.

CREDO CONFIRMATION WEBSITE

www.credoconfirmation.com

The *CREDO Confirmation* website at *www.credoconfirmation.com* has all of the reproducible handouts and additional information and activities related to the sessions and retreats that you will need. Prior to each session, make sure to print out the handouts and have them ready for your session.

Covenant and Expectations

Before your confirmation program begins, establish a confirmation covenant with your confirmands and their parents. A sample covenant is available at *www.credoconfirmation.com*. Be clear about the expectations that confirmands must meet and how these expectations relate to the confirmation vows.

SUGGESTED EXPECTATIONS FOR CONFIRMATION

attend all confirmation classes

While circumstances inevitably will arise that cause some confirmands to miss an occasional class (such as family emergencies), all participants and their parents need to understand that anyone wishing to be confirmed must make confirmation a priority. Be clear to families of confirmands that attendance is not optional. If a confirmand cannot attend a class because of an emergency, work with the confirmand, along with his or her parents and mentor, to make sure he or she gets any information that was missed.

attend worship each Sunday

Weekly worship is the most comprehensive way in which a congregation rehearses its faith and is recharged by God. Those wishing to take the confirmation vows and enter into a covenant with the body of Christ and with your congregation need to attend worship for most, if not all, of the Sundays for the duration of the confirmation program. While it is best for the confirmands to worship with the congregation in which they are being confirmed, it is more important that they develop weekly worship habits. If a confirmand splits time between two parents who attend two different churches, it is OK if he or she worships with one congregation one week and with another congregation the next. It also is OK for confirmands who are spending a weekend at the home of a friend or out-of-town family member to attend worship with their hosts. Consider requiring confirmands to attend worship at least three Sundays per month (allowing for exceptions in the case of family emergencies).

meet regularly with a mentor

You can find information on recruiting and training mentors in the "Mentoring and Confirmation" section of this resource. Be sure to adhere to your congregation or annual conference's Safe Sanctuaries standards where mentoring relationships are concerned. Also consider having confirmands and their mentors sit together in worship at least once per month.

participate in a christian education setting other than confirmation

This may not be possible if your confirmation classes meet during the Sunday school hour and your congregation has no other education opportunities for confirmation-age youth. (If this is the case, you might consider launching a mid-week small group ministry.) If your confirmation classes meet on Sunday afternoon or evening or during the week (and if your congregation offers Sunday school classes for confirmation-age youth), confirmands should get in the habit of attending Sunday school each week. Consider requiring confirmands to attend Sunday school at least three Sundays per month, possibly with the option of substituting a mid-week Bible study.

fulfill a service requirement

Service should be completed through the ministries of the congregation and can include participating in traditional service projects, helping with ministries to homeless and/or hungry persons, assisting with vacation Bible school, or serving as an acolyte or other worship leader. The number of service hours you require will vary depending on the service opportunities available to confirmands. But 8 hours—one hour per week for 8 weeks—is a good requirement.

attend a retreat and the prayer lock-in

Getting away from routines and familiar settings provides valuable opportunities for deep spiritual reflection and an intimate connection with God and others. This resource provides a confirmation retreat plan as well as a prayer-focused lock-in. Many United Methodist annual conferences and districts also host confirmation retreats that your group may be able to participate in. Make sure that your confirmation schedule includes either the retreat included here or a conference retreat so that your class gets the benefit of concentrated time away focused on their growing discipleship.

Creation, Sin, and Redemption

INTRODUCTION

To understand who we are, what we believe, and how we should live as Christians, we first have to know our story. Our story begins at the beginning, with God's creation of the heavens and earth. The accounts of Creation in the opening chapters of Genesis teach us that God created all things, created humankind in God's image, and declared all of Creation good.

In the third chapter of Genesis, sin enters the picture and everything changes. This story is familiar to confirmands who have grown up in the church. They know that in the middle of the garden is the tree from which Adam and Eve are forbidden to eat, that the serpent tempts Eve to take a bite of the forbidden fruit, and that Adam decides to do likewise. Confirmation gives youth an opportunity to go deeper and consider not only the consequences of sin for all people and how sin affects our relationships with God, with one another, and with all of Creation.

The good news is that sin doesn't have the last word. From the moment that sin entered Creation, God has been working to redeem and restore the world. In God's ultimate act of redemption, God—in the person of Jesus—became fully human and died on a cross. His death as "the perfect and sufficient sacrifice for the sins of the whole world, redeeming [humanity] from all sin" (Discipline, ¶ 103, Article VIII). Then, through his resurrection, Christ defeated death, giving us hope that one day we will experience resurrection and live eternally with God.

THREE IN ONE

In this story of creation, sin, and redemption, we see our triune God at work. ("Triune" is a fancy way to say "three-in-one.") In particular, we see God the Father, our Creator; and Jesus Christ, our Redeemer. (We'll focus on the person of the Holy Spirit, our Sustainer, in the next session.) The idea of a triune God can be difficult for young people to grasp. (For that matter, the Trinity can be a difficult concept for seminary-educated adults to grasp.)

What is easier to grasp is how each person of the Trinity relates to us. God the Father loves us as a parent and passes onto us God-like traits that we all possess—love, compassion, creativity, and so forth. Christ, our redeemer, can relate to us on a personal level because he became fully human and faced the same struggles and temptations that we face. And he suffered and died on our behalf, setting for us an incredible example of love and sacrifice. (We will focus on the Holy Spirit in the following session.)

all are broken, none are hopeless

Young people need to know that God created all things and declared all things "good." They also need to understand the reality of sin. Paul tells us, "All have sinned and fall short of God's glory" (**Romans 3:23**). We are all sinners; and we live in a sinful, broken world. We are all in need of redemption and reconciliation.

In human societies, the legal repercussions for breaking the rules can be strident and unyielding. Many youth attend schools that have "zero-tolerance" policies toward certain behaviors. Thus, it might be difficult for young people to believe that they can truly be forgiven for and redeemed of bad decisions and sinful choices. But God works differently. God's grace is always available to us, regardless of who we are or what we have done.

The good news of redemption should be delivered with gentleness and joy. Because of Christ's life, death, and resurrection, we are free to live without the burden of sins. **First Peter 2:24** says, "[Jesus] himself bore our sins in his body on the cross, so that, free from sins, we might live for righteousness." Jesus saves us *from* sin but saves us *for* a life lived in service to God and others.

SUPPLIES AND PREPARATION

BASIC SUPPLIES

- ☐ Bibles of various translations
- ☐ markerboard or large sheets of paper
- ☐ markers
- ☐ pens or pencils
- ☐ clear tape and/or glue
- ☐ masking tape
- ☐ index cards or paper cut about the same size (3-by-5 or 4-by-6)
- ☐ sheets of posterboard
- ☐ paper (Use paper that has already been used on one side as much as possible, depending on the activity.)
- ☐ scissors

ACTIVITY	PREPARATION	OTHER SUPPLIES
Opening Ritual	Create a "vine." Write the opening meditation—which is adapted from 1 Chronicles 16:8, 12, 15, 23—on a markerboard; or project the meditation, using the slide on the website.	☐ vine that will be added to each session ☐ vine branches (1 for each student)
Order of Creation	Make a copy of "Order of Creation" on the website. Cut the strips apart, and put each set in a separate envelope.	☐ 2 envelopes ☐ strips of paper cut from "Order of Creation"
Created in God's Image	Gather supplies.	
Back to the Beginning	Gather supplies.	
Re-Re-Redemption	Gather supplies.	
Our Redeemer	Gather 4 or 5 damaged items that could be repaired, such as a chair or small table with a broken leg, ripped clothes, or a broken toy that could be fixed with glue or screws.	☐ broken items that could be repaired
Redemption in the United Methodist Tradition	Gather supplies.	☐ *Book of Discipline*
Closing Ritual	Write the benediction, "John Wesley's Rule," on a markerboard; or print out the poster from the website.	

OPTIONAL VIDEOS

Creation		
Sin	Preview the videos.	☐ *Credo Confirmation Multimedia Teaching Tools* (the DVD) ☐ equipment with which to show the videos
Redemption		

OPENING RITUAL

(10 minutes)

supplies

❑ vine that will be added to each session
❑ vine branches (1 for each student)
❑ markers or pens

preparation: Create a "vine." Write the opening meditation—which is adapted from 1 Chronicles 16:8, 12, 15, 23—on a markerboard; or project the meditation, using the slide on the website.

Each session in CREDO begins with an opening ritual inspired by **John 15:1-9** ("I am the vine, you are the branches"—verse 5*a*). Prior to the first session, you will need to create a "vine." Draw a tree trunk on a large sheet of paper, paint a trunk on a wall in your meeting space, construct a vine or tree out of wood. Be creative, and involve the confirmands as much as possible. Also prior to the first session, you will need one "branch" for each confirmand (see below).

During the three sessions of first unit, "Know Your Story," the confirmands will add branches to the vine or trunk. During the second unit, "Confirm Your Faith," the confirmands will add leaves to the branches. And during the final unit, "Live Your Commitment," the confirmands will add fruit to the branches ("Those who abide in me and I in them bear much fruit"—**John 15:5*b***). Be creative in how you represent the branches, leaves, and fruit that grow from the vine or trunk.

As the confirmands arrive for the first session, give each person a branch or the means to make one. Invite each person to write on his or her branch something that he or she has gained from the time he or she has spent in the church so far. This might include knowledge gained from a Sunday school teacher, the love and support of an older member of the congregation, the friendship of fellow Christian young people, a relationship with God. Instruct the confirmands to attach their branches to the vine.

Say: "Jesus teaches, 'Just as the branch cannot bear fruit by itself unless it abides in the vine, neither can you unless you abide in me' (**John 15:4*b***). When we, the branches, abide in Christ, the vine, we are drawn into God's ongoing story. This story involves several people who are rooted in Christ and who have branched out into the world, touching people with God's love and grace."

When all of the confirmands have arrived, invite each person to talk briefly about what he or she wrote on his or her branch. Then invite the youth to read aloud the opening meditation (included on the website in the "Opening Meditations" handout), which is adapted from **1 Chronicles 16:8, 12, 15, 23**:

> Give thanks to the Lord,
> and make God's deeds known among the peoples.
> Remember the wonderful works that God has done;
> remember God's covenant forever.
> Sing to the Lord, all the earth.
> Tell of God's salvation every day.

video option: creation
(5–10 minutes)

If you have a copy of *Credo Confirmation Multimedia Teaching Tools,* open this session with the "Creation" video segment. This video gives the confirmands an overview of Creation and what it means for us to be made in God's image.

order of creation
(10 minutes)

Divide the confirmands into two groups, and give each group one of the two sets of slips cut from "Order of Creation" on the website. Give these groups three minutes to put the activities of creation in order without referring to the Bible.

After 3 minutes, ask the groups to tape their slips, in the agreed upon order, on a wall. Then ask volunteers to read aloud **Genesis 1:1–2:4a** and **2:4b–25** to check the groups' accuracy. (An answer key is available on the website.)

Ask:

❧ What is familiar to you about these Scriptures? What did you notice in these Scriptures that you hadn't noticed or thought about before?
❧ What do these Scriptures tell us about God? What do they tell us about the world God has created?

created in god's image
(15–20 minutes)

Ask a volunteer to read aloud **Genesis 1:27.** Then say: "This verse says that God created us in God's image. This doesn't necessarily mean that we physically look like God but means that we share many of God's characteristics."

Ask:

❧ What is something you have worked hard to create? (works of art, projects they have built or put together with their parents, a website they have constructed, and so forth)
❧ How do you feel about these creations? What have you done to protect or preserve them?

Say: "Like God, we have the ability to create and to care for our creations. Creativity is one important way in which we bear God's image."

Then say: "Since we are created in God's image, as we learn more about who God is, we learn more about who we are and whom God calls us to be."

Ask volunteers to read aloud each of the following Scriptures. Discuss with the class how each passage describes God.

Matthew 20:1-16 (*like a generous boss*)
Luke 15:8-10 (*like a rejoicing woman*)
Luke 15:11-32 (*like a forgiving father*)
John 10:1-18 (*like a shepherd*)
John 13:3-5, 12-16 (*like a servant*)

Divide the confirmands into groups of three or four. Ask each group to select one of the Scriptures above and to create a skit in which a person fits that Scripture's description of God. For example, using the description of God in **Matthew 20:1-16,** the youth might create a skit about a boss who brings out the best in his or her workers and goes out of his or her way to show appreciation for what the workers do. Or they might use the description of God in **Luke 15:11-32** to create a skit about a parent who loves and forgives (but doesn't necessarily excuse) a child even after that child betrays the parent's trust.

VIDEO OPTION: SIN
(5–10 minutes)

If you have a copy of *Credo Confirmation Multimedia Teaching Tools,* show the "Sin" video segment. This video gives the confirmands an overview of how sin damaged God's good creation and continues to be at work in our world today.

BACK TO THE BEGINNING
(10–15 minutes)

Ask the youth to turn in their Bible to **Genesis 3.** Ask volunteers to read aloud the Scripture, each person reading one verse at a time until the passage is complete.

Say: "This Scripture tells the story of sin entering God's Creation. Sin is our brokenness, our separation from God, our fractured world, and our need of healing."

Ask:

> ❧ Who sinned in this Scripture? What was sinful?
> ❧ What happened as a result of these sins? What relationships were hurt?

Say: "God created all things and declared all of Creation 'good.' But when sin enters the story, God's good creation is damaged."

Hand out paper and markers or color pencils and ask the confirmands to illustrate, by drawing or writing, one way in which sin has damaged some part of God's good creation. Encourage the confirmands to think not just about physical damage but also emotional and spiritual damage and damage done to relationships. Give everyone plenty of time to work, then invite the confirmands to present their illustrations and writings and to explain how sin has damaged Creation.

supplies
❑ *Credo Confirmation Multimedia Teaching Tools* (the DVD)
❑ equipment with which to show DVD videos

supplies
❑ Bibles
❑ paper
❑ color pencils or markers

video option: redemption

(5–10 minutes)

If you have a copy of *Credo Confirmation Multimedia Teaching Tools*, show the "Redemption" video segment. This video gives the confirmands an overview of how God, in Christ, heals creation and restores our relationship with God.

re-re-redemption

(10 minutes)

Ask:

❧ How would you define the word *redemption*?

❧ Where have you heard the word redemption before? (*They may have redeemed tickets for prizes at a redemption center at a fair or arcade or they may have heart redemption used to describe someone who has overcome a past mistake in judgment.*)

Say: "In biblical times redemption was often associated with slavery." Ask a volunteer to read aloud **Leviticus 25:47-49.** Explain that, in many ancient cultures, selling oneself into slavery was a way to pay off a debt. Redemption meant paying off one's debt—or having one's debt paid off by someone else—and being released.

Then ask a volunteer to read aloud **Romans 7:14-20.** Ask:

❧ What does it mean to be a slave to sin? How does sin keep people from being free?

Ask another volunteer to read aloud **Romans 8:1-8.** Ask:

❧ How can we be freed from slavery to sin?

Write and then read aloud the following definition of *redemption*:

Redemption: the state of being redeemed; deliverance form sin through the life, death, and resurrection of Christ

our redeemer

(10–15 minutes)

Preparation: Gather 4 or 5 damaged items that could be repaired

Say: "God the Father is the person of the Trinity who acts as our Creator. Another person of the Trinity, Jesus Christ, acts as our redeemer."

Read aloud **Romans 3:23:** "All have sinned and fall short of God's glory."

Say: "Because we are all sinners, we all need redemption."

Present to the confirmands some of the broken items that you gathered beforehand. For each item, ask:

➤ How could you fix this item?
➤ When we fix this item, will it be as good as it was before it was broken? Will it be better than it was before it was broken?

Then ask:

➤ How does God, through Christ, "fix" us?

To answer this question, have the youth read these Scriptures:

➤ **Romans 5:6-9:** Paul says, "We have been justified by [Christ's] blood" (verse 9). This likely alludes to the ancient Jewish practice of making blood sacrifices to atone for sins. See Leviticus 4:1–5:13 for information on making sacrifices to atone for sins. ("To atone" means to make amends or make things right.)
➤ **Romans 5:12-15, 18-19:** Paul says that, since human beings brought sin into the world, a human being—Jesus—must make atonement for the sins of humankind and put human beings back into a right relationship with God.
➤ **Romans 6:1-11:** Paul says that Christ, through his death, destroyed the power of sin. Through Christ's resurrection, Christ destroyed the power of death. Paul says that we are baptized into Christ's death so that we can share in Christ's resurrection.
➤ **1 Peter 2:24:** Not only did Jesus save us from our sins by dying on the cross, but Jesus also saved us for a life of righteousness.

After each Scripture, ask:

➤ What does this Scripture tell us about Christ, how Christ is our redeemer, and how Christ atones, or makes amends, for our sins? (You might need to assist in this discussion, using the notes next to each Scripture reference, above.)
➤ What questions does this Scripture raise for you about how Christ saves us from sin? What is unclear to you about this Scripture?

Say: "As Christians, we believe that Jesus, through his death and resurrection, atoned for our sins and made us right with God. Because of what Jesus has done, we can look forward to living eternally with God."

redemption in the United Methodist Tradition
(5–10 minutes)

Ask a volunteer to read aloud "Article VIII—Reconciliation Through Christ" from "The Confession of Faith of the Evangelical United Brethren Church" under "Our Doctrinal

supplies
❑ Bibles of various translations
❑ 4 or 5 damaged items

preparation: Gather 4 or 5 damaged items that could be repaired, such as a chair or small table with a broken leg, ripped clothes, or a broken toy that could be fixed with glue or screws.

supplies
☐ *The Book of Discipline*

NOTE: Before you dismiss, instruct the confirmands to read, reflect on, and journal about the material in the "Creation," "Sin," and "Redemption" sections of the CREDO STUDENT JOURNAL before your next session. Also encourage them to try to do the activities related to "Creation," "Sin," and "Redemption" on the confirmand website at *www.credoconfirmation.com*.

supplies
☐ markerboard
☐ marker

preparation: Write the benediction, "John Wesley's Rule," on a markerboard; or print out the poster from the website.

Standards and General Rules" in *The Book of Discipline of The United Methodist Church*. This statement also is available below and at the website.

Explain that the Evangelical United Brethren Church was one of two denominations that merged in 1968 to form The United Methodist Church. (The other was the Methodist Church.)

We believe God was in Christ reconciling the world to himself. The offering Christ freely made on the cross is the perfect and sufficient sacrifice for the sins of the whole world, redeeming man from all sin, so that no other satisfaction is required.

Say: "This statement affirms that Christ is our redeemer and that Christ is capable of atoning for the sins of the entire world."

Allow the confirmands to ask questions, and help them understand the language used in this statement.

Then ask:

- What does it mean that Christ's sacrifice is "perfect and sufficient"?
- How can this statement give us hope and comfort when we struggle with sin?

CLOSING RITUAL
(5 minutes)

Gather the confirmands into a circle. Lead the youth in prayer, giving thanks to God for your time together and all that the group has learned and experienced. Then go around the circle, inviting each person to pray aloud one word or phrase that describes something he or she learned during the past week of confirmation.

After every person has had a chance to contribute a word or phrase, say a brief closing prayer. Then invite the confirmands to say about and in unison the benediction, "John Wesley's Rule":

> Do all the good you can,
> By all the means you can,
> In all the ways you can,
> In all the places you can,
> At all the times you can,
> To all the people you can,
> As long as ever you can.

Note: Although we traditionally attribute this saying to John Wesley, there is no evidence that Wesley ever actually said it. Still, Wesley's Rule has been a popular saying among United Methodists for decades and serves as a great summary of how to live our lives in response to Wesley's second General Rule, "Do good."

A Church Empowered by the Holy Spirit

INTRODUCTION

You may be familiar with this rhyme and finger play: "Here is the church. Here is the steeple. Open the doors, and see all the people." (Go ahead and do the finger motions. We'll wait.)

The problem with this finger play is that it equates the church with a building. An alternative ending to the rhyme— "Open the doors, and where are the people?"—even implies that the church can exist without the people. In reality, the church is the people, dictionary definitions notwithstanding. The people may own a building with a steeple on top, but they are greater than the sum of their real estate.

I AM THE CHURCH, YOU ARE THE CHURCH, WE ARE THE CHURCH TOGETHER

So how should we define church. Here's what The Book of Discipline of The United Methodist Church says in the Preamble to the Constitution:

> The church is a community of all true believers under the Lordship of Christ. It is the redeemed and redeeming fellowship in which the Word of God is preached by persons divinely called, and the sacraments are duly administered according to Christ's own appointment. Under the discipline of the Holy Spirit the church seeks to provide for the maintenance of worship, the edification of believers, and the redemption of the world.

It's a dense definition, but it explains who the church is and why it exists. It also tells us that the church is "under the discipline of the Holy Spirit."

SO WHO IS THE HOLY SPIRIT?

Of the three Persons of the Trinity, the Holy Spirit tends to be the hardest for us to understand. We understand God the Father, the Creator, because we encounter this person of the Trinity in the Creation narratives, during conversations with Abraham and Moses, in Israel's deliverance from slavery and exile, and elsewhere in Scripture. We understand Christ because he became fully human as Jesus. Jesus experienced all of the suffering and temptation that come with being human.

But the Holy Spirit? The Spirit is much more difficult to relate to. This Person of the Trinity is as hard to hold on to as the wind, which is appropriate because the Hebrew and Greek words for "Spirit," ruach and pneuma respectively, also mean "wind" and "breath."

Jesus in John 14:26 describes the Holy Spirit as an Advocate, Counselor, or Companion (depending on the translation). Jesus tells his disciples that the Spirit "will teach you everything, and remind you of all that I have said to you" (NRSV). But the Spirit is much more than an angel sitting on our shoulder and helping us make tough decisions. The Spirit also empowers us (Acts 4:31), blesses us with spiritual gifts (1 Corinthians 12:1-11), and prays for us in "sighs too deep for words" when we don't know the words to pray (Romans 8:26, NRSV).

The Holy Spirit empowers the church—God's people—to do the work of God's kingdom. While we often equate the kingdom of God with heaven and eternity, it isn't so remote. In fact, when asked when the kingdom is coming, Jesus said, "God's kingdom is already among you" (Luke 17:21, CEB). As the church, we are not just focused on some future reality. We can do God's work right here and right now.

SUPPLIES AND PREPARATION

BASIC SUPPLIES

- ❑ Bibles of various translations
- ❑ markerboard or large sheets of paper
- ❑ markers
- ❑ pens or pencils

- ❑ clear tape and/or glue
- ❑ masking tape
- ❑ index cards or paper cut about the same size (3-by-5 or 4-by-6)
- ❑ sheets of posterboard

- ❑ paper (Use paper that has already been used on one side as much as possible, depending on the activity.)
- ❑ scissors

ACTIVITY	PREPARATION	OTHER SUPPLIES
Opening Ritual	Write the opening meditation—which is adapted from 1 Chronicles 16:8, 12, 15, 23—on a markerboard; or project the meditation, using the slide on the website.	❑ vine from previous sessions ❑ vine branches (1 for each student)
The Spirit in Scripture	Gather supplies.	❑ optional: Bible with pronunciations in it or an audio Bible and equipment to play it on
Defining Church	Gather supplies.	❑ optional: *The Book of Discipline of The United Methodist Church*
The Spirit Moving in You	Be prepared to tell the youth an example from your own life about the Spirit nudging you. (See the activity.)	
The Spirit Moving in John Wesley	Make copies of the "Spirit Moving in John Wesley" worksheet and narrative on the website.	❑ "Spirit Moving in John Wesley" worksheet and narrative
Forefathers, Mothers, and Others	Make copies of and cut apart the "Forefathers, Mothers, and Others Biographies" handout and "Forefathers, Mothers, and Others Cards" on the website.	❑ "Forefathers, Mothers, and Others Biographies" handout ❑ "Forefathers, Mothers, and Others Cards"
The Members of the Body	Gather supplies.	
Closing Ritual	Write the benediction, "John Wesley's Rule," on a markerboard; or print out the poster from the website.	

OPTIONAL VIDEOS

Holy Spirit Church	Preview the videos.	❑ *Credo Confirmation Multimedia Teaching Tools* (the DVD) ❑ equipment with which to show the videos

❏ vine that will be added to each session
❏ vine branches (1 for each student)
❏ markers or pens

preparation: Have on hand supplies for the youth to add branches to the vine. Write the opening meditation—which is adapted from 1 Chronicles 16:8, 12, 15, 23—on a markerboard; or project the meditation, using the slide on the website.

note: Take time before you get started to talk with the confirmands about what they read and wrote in the "Creation," "Sin," and "Redemption" sections of their CREDO STUDENT JOURNALS.

supplies

❏ *Credo Confirmation Multimedia Teaching Tools* (the DVD)
❏ equipment with which to show DVD videos

opening ritual
(10 minutes)

As confirmands arrive, point them to the confirmation vine (see the "Creation, Sin, and Redemption" session, page 17) and give each person a branch. Invite the confirmands to reflect on the previous session and to write on their branch something they learned or experienced during that session. Ask the confirmands to attach their branch to the vine. Remind the youth that this vine and its branches represent God's story, a story that they are a part of.

When all of the confirmands have arrived, invite each person to talk briefly about what he or she wrote on his or her branch. Then invite the youth to read aloud the opening meditation, which is adapted from **1 Chronicles 16:8, 12, 15, 23:**

> Give thanks to the Lord,
>   and make God's deeds known among the peoples.
> Remember the wonderful works that God has done;
>   remember God's covenant forever.
> Sing to the Lord, all the earth.
>   Tell of God's salvation every day.

video option: holy spirit
(5–10 minutes)

If you have a copy of *Credo Confirmation Multimedia Teaching Tools,* show the "Holy Spirit" video segment. This video gives the confirmands an overview of who the Holy Spirit is and how the Spirit is at work among us.

the spirit in scripture
(10 minutes)

Say: "In the previous session, as we talked about creation, we took a close look at God the Father, or Creator. Then, as we discussed redemption, we talked about God the Son, Jesus Christ, our Redeemer. In this session, we'll meet God the Holy Spirit."

Divide the confirmands into pairs or groups of three. Assign one or more of the Scriptures below to each group. (It's OK if multiple groups look at the same Scriptures, but make sure that every Scripture is assigned to at least one group.) Give each group a few minutes to read its Scripture(s) and to discuss what the passage says about the Holy Spirit.

Genesis 1:1-5 (The Spirit is present at Creation.)
Matthew 3:13-17 (The Spirit descends on Jesus at his baptism.)
John 14:25-27 (The Spirit is our teacher and advocate.)
Romans 5:1-5 (The Spirit fills our hearts with love.)
Romans 8:26-27 (The Spirit intercedes and prays for us.)
1 Corinthians 12:1-11 (The Spirit blesses us with spiritual gifts.)

Bring everyone back together and ask each group to summarize, in a single sentence, its Scripture and what the passage has to say about the Holy Spirit. Write these summaries on a markerboard.

Then say: "There is one very important Scripture about the Holy Spirit that we didn't cover: the story of Pentecost."

Invite volunteers to read aloud **Acts 2:1-21.** An adult may need to read verses 9–11 (and rehearse beforehand) because of the difficult names. (You might also consider using an audio Bible.)

Ask the confirmands to listen carefully to what the Scripture says about who the Holy Spirit is and what the Holy Spirit does. Ask the youth to name these things aloud. List their responses on a markerboard.

Say: "Nowadays, we celebrate Pentecost—the day on which the Holy Spirit descended on Jesus' disciples—as the birthday of the church. Some congregations even serve birthday cake on Pentecost Sunday."

video option: church
(5–10 minutes)

If you have a copy of *Credo Confirmation Multimedia Teaching Tools,* show the "Church" video segment. This video gives the confirmands an overview of what the church is and what it means for us to be part of the church.

defining church
(5–10 minutes)

Say: "We think of Pentecost as the church's birthday, but what is the church?" Point out that defining church isn't as easy as it might seem.

Ask the confirmands to spend a few minutes brainstorming words and short phrases that describe or define *church,* as you list them on a markerboard. Once you have a good list, have the confirmands work together, using the words and phrases they've identified, to come up with a good definition of *church.*

Possible definitions might include the following:

"A group of people who love God and come together to worship, learn about God, and serve God's people"

"A congregation, or body of people, united together in the service of God" (This is John Wesley's definition, from this "Of the Church" sermon.)

Then read aloud the definition of church that is in the Preamble to the Constitution in *The Book of Discipline:*

supplies
❏ Bibles
❏ scratch paper (preferably paper that has been used on one side already)
❏ pens or pencils
❏ markerboard
❏ marker
❏ optional: Bible with pronunciations in it or an audio Bible and equipment to play it on

supplies
❏ *Credo Confirmation Multimedia Teaching Tools* (the DVD)
❏ equipment with which to show DVD videos

supplies
❏ markerboard
❏ marker
❏ optional: *The Book of Discipline of The United Methodist Church*

The church is a community of all true believers under the Lordship of Christ. It is the redeemed and redeeming fellowship in which the Word of God is preached by persons divinely called, and the sacraments are duly administered according to Christ's own appointment. Under the discipline of the Holy Spirit the church seeks to provide for the maintenance of worship, the edification of believers, and the redemption of the world.

preparation: Be prepared to tell the youth an example from your own life about the Spirit nudging you.

THE SPIRIT MOVING IN YOU

(10 minutes)

Say: "As members of Christ's holy church, we are empowered by the Holy Spirit. The books of the Bible were originally written in Hebrew and Greek. The Hebrew word for spirit— *ruach* (ROO-ah)—and the Greek word for spirit—*pneuma* (NOO-muh)—also mean 'wind' and 'breath.'"

Invite the confirmands to breathe gently on the backs of their hands.

Say: "The Holy Spirit is the breath of God that fills us with life. We see this image of the Spirit in **Genesis 2:7,** when God breathes life into Adam's nostrils."

Then turn on a small fan that has streamers tied to its grill.

Point out the fan, and say: "The Holy Spirit, like the wind, is invisible but powerful, moving things around as it wills."

Then invite a youth to read aloud **John 3:8:** "The wind blows where it chooses, and you hear the sound of it, but you do not know where it comes from or where it goes. So it is with everyone who is born of the Spirit."

Ask:

- Have you ever traveled in a wind-powered vehicle such as a sailboat or hot-air balloon?
- When traveling by sailboat or hot-air balloon, what determines your course? (the wind)
- What role does the captain or operator of these vehicles play? (understanding and cooperating with the wind, not fighting against it)
- Does the wind sometimes take the boat or balloon where the captain or operator doesn't want to go? (yes)
- How is the Holy Spirit similar to the wind? (The Spirit guides our path; the Spirit sometimes pushes us in directions we don't feel comfortable going; it's easier to go with the Spirit than against the Spirit; and so on.)

Then ask the confirmands whether they have ever felt pulled, perhaps by the Spirit, to do something that they didn't really want to do. This might be anything from being nice to an annoying sibling to reaching out to someone at school whom others ignore or abuse.

Be prepared to tell the youth an example from your life, perhaps about the Spirit nudging you into a line of work that you hadn't previously considered, pushing you to sacrifice something that you enjoyed but knew that you could do without, or instructing you to make changes in the way you budget your time and/or money.

THE SPIRIT MOVING IN JOHN WESLEY

(15 minutes)

Tell the confirmands that you will tell them a story about how the Holy Spirit touched the life of John Wesley, a founder of the Methodist movement, but that you're going to let them help tell the story in the style of Mad Libs™.

If you have a large group, divide the youth into groups of 3 or 4. Then give each group a copy of the "Spirit Moving in John Wesley" worksheet from the website. Give the teams a few minutes to fill out their worksheets. Then read aloud "The Spirit Moving in John Wesley Narrative" from the website, filling in one group's words as you go. Read the story again, using another group's words.

Continue until all of the groups have been represented. Finally, read aloud the story, using the correct words.

Then ask:

- ❧ When, in this story, was the Holy Spirit working in John Wesley's life? (all of the time)
- ❧ When, in this story, might John Wesley have been resisting or working against the Spirit? (when he tried to reduce faith to a set of rules; when we went to Georgia even though he wasn't prepared)
- ❧ When did John Wesley allow the Spirit to lead him? (when we learned from the Moravians; when he went to the meeting on Aldersgate Street; as he kept wrestling with what it means to be a Christian)
- ❧ Why, do you think, was John Wesley's experience on Aldersgate Street so powerful?

Then ask confirmands to think of a time when they went to an event or took on an activity reluctantly or with low expectations but, to their surprise, had a positive or even life-changing experience. This might have been when they watched a movie that they found themselves thinking about for days (or that made them cry) or a church retreat where they heard God speaking to them. Allow volunteers to tell about their experiences, and be prepared to tell a story from your experience.

Say: "The meeting that John Wesley went to on Aldersgate Street was pretty ordinary. It was the sort of meeting that happened frequently. The same can be said for Pentecost. Pentecost is another name for the Jewish holiday Shavuot (shuh-VOO-oht), an annual celebration that recalls the event when God gave Moses and the Israelites the Torah on Mt.

supplies
❑ pens or pencils
❑ copies of "Spirit Moving in John Wesley" worksheets

preparation: Make copies of the worksheet for small groups of youth and a copy of the narrative for yourself.

Sinai. What was different about that particular meeting on Aldersgate Street and that particular Pentecost celebration was the way that the Holy Spirit made something ordinary into something quite extraordinary."

supplies
❑ "Forefathers, Mothers, and Others Biographies" handout
❑ "Forefathers, Mothers, and Others Cards"

preparation: Make copies of the "Forefathers, Mothers, and Others Biographies" handout and "Forefathers, Mothers, and Others Cards" on the website. Cut apart the cards so that each box on the grid is a separate card.

FOREFATHERS, MOTHERS, AND OTHERS

(5–10 minutes)

Say: "The Holy Spirit has worked through countless people—some well-known and others anonymous—who have made The United Methodist Church what it is today. We're going to take a quick look at four of these persons.

Hand out copies of the biographies of the following four persons from the website:

Francis Asbury
Barbara Heck
John Stewart
William Wadé Harris

Give the confirmands a few minutes to read over the biographies. While they're doing this, spread out on the floor, face down, the 20 cards cut from the "Forefathers, Mothers, and Others" handout from the website. Have the confirmands leave the biographies handout behind as they move to the floor to work together to match the cards to the person whom they describe. Give them plenty of time to work, then check their answers against the information on the biographies handout.

THE MEMBERS OF THE BODY

(15 minutes)

Tell the confirmands that they'll be taking a pop quiz.

supplies
❑ scratch paper
❑ pens and pencils

Distribute scratch paper, and ask the confirmands to write down two numbers: the number of ministers in your congregation and the number of people it takes to put on a worship service in your congregation. (Do not differentiate between ministers and pastors at this time.)

Ask volunteers to give their answers to these two questions, but don't indicate whether the answers are right or wrong.

Say: "Let's work together to figure out how many people it takes to put on a worship service in our congregation."

Invite volunteers to call out a specific job (for example, "preach the sermon," "select the hymns," or "clean the sanctuary") and how many people do that job for the worship service. List these jobs and the number of people required to do them on a markerboard. Don't worry if the youth don't know precise numbers (such as how many choir members there are). Just write down a rough estimate and move on.

When the youth have run out of ideas, suggest additional jobs from the following list, modifying it to fit your church's structure:

pastor
liturgist
music director
musicians
sound/video technicians
ushers
greeters
custodians or others who prepare the worship space
parking lot attendants
whoever prepares and reproduces the worship bulletins
nursery workers
children's church coordinator and workers

Add the numbers to get a grand total. Regardless of your church's size, this should be a fairly large number relative to worship attendance.

Then ask:

❧ In addition to worship, what are some things that our congregation does? (*outreach in the community and around the world, care for members of the congregation who are ill or grieving, providing educational opportunities, and so forth*)

Ask the confirmands to name some of the persons who are involved in each of these ministries of the church. Offer help as needed.

Return to the first question and ask whether any of the confirmands would like to revise his or her answers to the first question (the number of ministers in your congregation). Chances are good that at least one student will realize that the number of ministers in your congregations is a lot larger than the number of ordained clergy.

Discuss these questions:

❧ How many people listed on the board are ministers? (all of them)
❧ How many people in our congregation are ministers? (all who play a role in carrying out the work of the church—whether in worship or in their day-to-day lives)
❧ How many people in our congregation are called to be ministers? (all of them)

Point out two or three of the ministry roles you've talked about that some people might consider "lesser" jobs. Talk about what would happen if these jobs didn't get done. (For example, without nursery workers, families with small children might not attend worship or be involved in certain ministries of the church, not to mention the ministry that

supplies
❏ markerboard
❏ marker

preparation: Write the benediction, "John Wesley's Rule" (on page 22), on a markerboard; or print out the poster from the website.

takes place between nursery workers and the children for whom they are caring. Without someone to print bulletins or project content on video screens, worshipers wouldn't know what to say or sing.)

Say: "Church is not like a play or concert, where you pay money to see a performance. Church is more like a team sport, where everybody has a job to do and every job is critical to the team's success."

CLOSING RITUAL
(5 minutes)

Gather the confirmands into a circle. Lead the youth in prayer, giving thanks to God for your time together and all that the group has learned and experienced. Then go around the circle, inviting each person to pray aloud one word or phrase that describes something he or she learned during the past week of confirmation.

After every person has had a chance to contribute a word or phrase, say a brief closing prayer. Then invite the confirmands to say about and in unison the benediction, "John Wesley's Rule."

Made New in Christ

INTRODUCTION

Quick! How many Creation stories are in the Bible? Casual observers will say one. Those who have read Genesis carefully (and Bible scholars who have practices source criticism) will say two: the one where God creates the world in six days and rests on the seventh (**Genesis 1:1–2:3**) and the one where God forms Adam and Eve in the Garden and gives them basic instructions for how to live (**Genesis 2:4-25**). Those who know the Bible cover to cover—or who have skipped ahead—will add a third Creation story: the one where God creates a new heaven and a new earth and the end of days (**Revelation 21:1–22:5**).

An even more careful reading of Scripture will reveal even more Creation stories. Over and over again, we encounter people who are made new through Christ. When Jesus dined with Matthew, the tax collector, Matthew left behind his sinful life and became one of Jesus' twelve disciples (**Matthew 9:9-13; 10:1-3**). The Samaritan woman whom Jesus met at the well, despite living a difficult life, went away from her meeting with Jesus overjoyed, and told everyone in her hometown that she'd met the Messiah (**John 4:4-42**). The criminal who was crucified next to Jesus repented as he was dying. Jesus told him, "Today you will be with me in Paradise" (**Luke 23:43**).

FULLY DIVINE, and FULLY HUMAN

As Christians, we believe that Jesus is both fully human and fully divine. Christ, the Son, is a person of the Trinity who was present at creation and who redeems us by defeating sin and death. But this redemption is possible because Jesus became fully human. Jesus lived on earth as an actual person. He faced temptation; he felt pain; he could enjoy a good meal or pleasant weather; he had blood pressure and a pulse. And he died a real death.

Jesus understands what it means to be human. He knows our pain, our suffering, our insecurity, and our joy. Jesus not only taught us how to live, he also set an example for us. And he wants to be in relationship with us.

a RELATIONSHIP WITH JESUS

Adolescence is a time of identify formation, when youth strive for belonging and seek to express themselves in new ways. Youth need healthy relationships with both peers and adults as they determine who they are, what they believe, and how they should live their lives. More importantly, they need to be in relationship with Jesus.

Being in a relationship with Jesus means fully trusting in him. It means spending time with him, in prayer and by reading and studying his teachings in Scripture. It means being ready and willing to tell other people about our relationship with him. It means being mindful of Jesus' promise in **Matthew 28:20:** "I myself will be with you every day until the end of the present age."

SUPPLIES AND PREPARATION

BASIC SUPPLIES

- ☐ Bibles of various translations
- ☐ markerboard or large sheets of paper
- ☐ markers
- ☐ pens or pencils

- ☐ clear tape and/or glue
- ☐ masking tape
- ☐ index cards or paper cut about the same size (3-by-5 or 4-by-6)
- ☐ sheets of posterboard

- ☐ paper (Use paper that has already been used on one side as much as possible, depending on the activity.)
- ☐ scissors

ACTIVITY	PREPARATION	OTHER SUPPLIES
Opening Ritual	Write the opening meditation—which is adapted from 1 Chronicles 16:8, 12, 15, 23—on a markerboard; or project the meditation, using the slide on the website.	☐ vine from previous sessions ☐ vine branches (1 for each student)
Who Is Jesus?	Gather supplies.	
Old Creatures, New Creations	Optional: Have on hand extra adult leaders.	☐ optional: extra adult leaders
Transformed and Transforming	Gather supplies.	
Changed		
He/She/They		
Closing Ritual	Write the benediction, "John Wesley's Rule," on a markerboard; or print out the poster from the website.	

OPTIONAL VIDEO

New Creation	Preview the video.	☐ *Credo Confirmation Multimedia Teaching Tools* (the DVD) ☐ equipment with which to show the video

- vine from previous sessions
- vine branches (1 for each student)
- markers or pens

preparation: Have on hand supplies for the youth to add branches to the vine. Write the opening meditation—which is adapted from 1 Chronicles 16:8, 12, 15, 23—on a markerboard; or project the meditation, using the slide on the website.

note: Take time before you get started to talk with the confirmands about what they read and wrote in the "Church" and "Holy Spirit" sections of their CREDO STUDENT JOURNALS.

supplies

- Bibles
- paper and half sheets of paper
- pens and pencils

Opening Ritual
(10 minutes)

As confirmands arrive, point them to the confirmation vine (see the "Creation" session, page 4) and give each person a branch. Invite the confirmands to reflect on the previous session and to write on their branch something they learned or experienced during that session. Ask the confirmands to attach their branch to the vine. Remind the youth that this vine and its branches represent God's story, a story that they are a part of.

When all of the confirmands have arrived, invite each person to talk briefly about what he or she wrote on his or her branch. Then invite the youth to read aloud the opening meditation, which is adapted from **1 Chronicles 16:8, 12, 15, 23:**

Give thanks to the Lord,
    and make God's deeds known among the peoples.
Remember the wonderful works that God has done;
    remember God's covenant forever.
Sing to the Lord, all the earth.
    Tell of God's salvation every day.

Who Is Jesus?
(15–20 minutes)

Divide the confirmands into pairs or groups of three. Make sure that each group has a sheet of paper and something to write with. Challenge the groups to complete the sentence "Jesus is" with as many different words as possible. These words could be adjectives (*wise, brave, loving*), titles (*Messiah, Redeemer, Son of God*), or descriptions that Jesus used for himself ("living water," "bread of life"). There are no limits to the words that groups can use, but the groups should be prepared to explain briefly why they selected a certain word.

Give the groups a couple minutes to work then invite a representative from each group to read aloud the group's list. (If you would like to make this activity competitive, you could award a point for each unique answer and declare the group with the most unique answers the winner.)

Then have volunteers read aloud each of the following Scriptures:

- **Matthew 9:1-8** (Jesus forgives then heals a paralyzed man.)
- **Luke 4:16-30** (Jesus preaches in his hometown synagogue.)
- **John 8:1-11** (Jesus responds to Pharisees who are preparing to stone an adulterous woman.)
- **John 13:2-17** (Jesus washes his disciples' feet.)

After each question, ask:

> ❥ What does this Scripture tell us about who Jesus is?

Hand out half sheets of paper and pens or pencils. Then ask:

> ❥ If someone were to ask you, "Who is Jesus?" how would you respond?

Instruct the confirmands to write their answers to this question on the half-sheets of paper. Give them a few minutes to work then invite each person to read aloud what he or she has written.

Video Option: new creation
(5–10 minutes)

If you have a copy of *Credo Confirmation Multimedia Teaching Tools*, show the "New Creation" video segment. This video gives the confirmands an overview of what it means for us to be made new in Christ.

Old creatures, new creations
(15 minutes)

Read aloud (or ask volunteers to read aloud) **Revelation 21:1-5; 22:1-15.**

Say: "These verses from the final chapters of the Book of Revelation tell the story of God making all things new. But we don't need to wait to experience God's new Creation. God is always making things new—including individuals. Let's look at some persons who became new creations when they encountered Jesus."

Assign each of the Scriptures below to a small group of youth. If possible, assign an adult leader to each group to help the confirmands better understand their assigned Scripture.

> ❥ **John 4:1-42** (the Samaritan woman at the well)
> ❥ **Luke 19:1-10** (Zacchaeus)
> ❥ **Acts 9:1-19** (Saul's conversion—Point out that Saul was also known as Paul.)

Have each group read the assigned Scripture and discuss the following questions:

> ❥ Who was changed?
> ❥ Why did he or she need to be changed?
> ❥ How did Jesus transform him or her?
> ❥ What happened next?

Give the youth a few minutes to work. Then have each person or group report on his, her, or their assigned Scripture.

Point out that, while the Bible tells several stories of people transformed by an encounter with Christ, these stories are not

supplies
- ❏ *Credo Confirmation Multimedia Teaching Tools* (the DVD)
- ❏ equipment with which to show DVD videos

supplies
- ❏ Bibles
- ❏ paper
- ❏ pens and pencils
- ❏ optional: extra adult leaders

preparation:
Optional: Have on hand extra adult leaders.

limited to Scripture. Christians throughout history (and today) have been made new in Christ. Remind the youth of John Wesley's Aldersgate experience, which they learned about in the previous session. Also emphasize that transformation doesn't happen in a single moment. Many people are made new gradually, over the course of their lives. And even those who have a dramatic conversion experience continue to grow and change long after their initial experience with Christ.

Transformed and Transforming
(10 minutes)

Explain that Paul (called Saul in **Acts 9:1-19**, in the previous activity) helped spread Christianity throughout the Roman Empire and wrote many letters that are included in the New Testament.

Read aloud **2 Corinthians 5:17** from three translations:

—New International Version: "Therefore, if anyone is in Christ, he is a new creation; the old has gone, the new has come!"

—New Revised Standard Version: "So if anyone is in Christ, there is a new creation: everything old has passed away; see, everything has become new!"

—Common English Bible: "So then, if anyone is in Christ, that person is part of the new creation. The old things have gone away, and look, new things have arrived."

Ask:

➤ What is the difference between these three versions? (*The NIV uses the word he; the NRSV uses there; the CEB uses is part of.*)

Say: "When someone has a relationship with Christ, he or she is made new. But that new creation is not limited to an individual person. When one person is transformed by Christ, that person—through his or her attitude and behavior—transforms those whom he or she encounters. There is a new creation: It starts with the individual, but it doesn't end with the individual. The individual is part of something bigger."

Ask:

➤ How does God use persons such as the woman at the well and Paul and Zacchaeus to transform others? (*The woman at the well told the people in her town about Jesus, and many believed because of her testimony. Paul became an important leader of the church, took the gospel message to many places throughout the Roman world, and wrote several letters included in the New Testament that have touched people's lives for nearly 2,000 years. Zacchaeus set an important example by repenting of his sins and promising to live differently.*)

CHANGED
(15 minutes)

Say: "We see in Scripture how people are transformed by their encounters with Jesus. We, too, change as a result of our relationship with Jesus."

Give the confirmands a minute or two to reflect on how their faith and their relationship with Jesus has transformed them. Then gather everyone into a circle. Go around the circle, and have each person introduce himself or herself by saying his or her name and one way in which he or she has been changed by Jesus. For example, "My name is Jimmy, and Jesus has made me more patient." Or "My name is Anna; and because of Jesus, I spend more time in prayer."

Allow youth to pass. Consider doing this activity again in future sessions, giving the youth more opportunities to name ways that Jesus has changed them.

SHE/HE/THEY
(20–25 minutes)

supplies
❑ markerboard
❑ marker

Divide the participants into groups of 3 or 4. Ask everyone to think of a person (or persons) who has had an impact on his or her faith journey and has helped him or her become who he or she is today. Have members of each group talk about the persons they chose and why they chose those persons.

Then write on a markerboard the following sentence: "She/He/They _____ me."

Ask the participants to complete the sentence above with the person(s) they named in mind. For example, "She loved me," "He taught me," or "They accepted me." They may also complete the sentence with short phrases, such as "He laughed with me," "She expected a lot from me," or "They prayed for me." (Hint: Past-tense verbs will fit better with all of the subjects. For example: The past tense of "She/He/They loved me" works better than "She/He/They loves me." The present-tense verb, in this instance, won't work with *they*, which would need to be *love,* instead.)

List their responses on the markerboard. Invite the group to repeat the sentence aloud and together: "They _____ me," over and over again, each time filling the blank with each of the words and phrases on the list.

Then write on the markerboard "Jesus _____ me." Again, lead the group in repeating the sentence aloud and together. This time fill in each blank with the present-tense version of the words and phrases on the list. For instance, "Jesus loves me," "Jesus teaches me," "Jesus expects a lot from me," and so on. The reason behind changing the words and phrases from past tense to present tense is because Jesus is living and active in the present.

Talk about any words or phrases that might not apply to Jesus, and discuss why they might not apply. Then ask:

❧ How does Jesus do all of these things with us and for us?
❧ Often Jesus does things with us and for us through other people. What does incarnation mean? (God in the flesh)

Say: "Usually, when we talk about incarnation, we are talking about God becoming human in the person of Jesus. While God is present in Jesus in a very unique way—Jesus was both fully divine and fully human—God continues to be present in the flesh of many people."

Then write on the markerboard a third sentence, "I will _____ others." Again lead the group in repeating the sentence aloud and together, filling in the blanks with the future-tense version of the words and phrases on the list. For example: "I will love others," "I will teach others," "I will pray for others."

CLOSING RITUAL
(5 minutes)

Gather the confirmands into a circle. Lead the youth in prayer, giving thanks to God for your time together and all that the group has learned and experienced. Then go around the circle, inviting each person to pray aloud one word or phrase that describes something he or she learned during the past week of confirmation.

After every person has had a chance to contribute a word or phrase, say a brief closing prayer. Then invite the confirmands to say about and in unison the benediction, "John Wesley's Rule."

Grace and the Way of Salvation

A center point of United Methodist theology is our Wesleyan understanding of grace. We affirm that salvation comes entirely through God's grace and that God's grace is with us throughout our lives and at every stage of our faith journey.

Grace can be defined as God's favor or as a gift from God that we have done nothing to earn. But a more complete definition of grace would be the way in which we experience God's extraordinary love and forgiveness.

prevenient grace

John Wesley identified three movements of grace, each of which has significant implications for ministry. The first movement is "prevenient grace." This is the grace of God that is present in all of our lives, even before we are aware of it. God constantly seeks each of us, through other people, through our experiences, and through our consciences. Those of us who are in ministry with young people must always remember that God's grace is present in and with children and youth, even those who are not active in church. Parents, teachers, congregation members, coaches...and you!...are agents of God's grace for youth. For young people, many of whom yearn for meaningful relationships, the knowledge that God is seeking them out is good news!

Justifying grace

Justifying grace is the second movement of grace. For many Christians, this is the most familiar form of grace. Justifying grace is the grace that brings us into right relationship with God. This, too, is a gift of God, who has acted in and through the life of Jesus. Our responsibility is to respond to God's grace in faith, to make a decision for Christ. Our ministries with youth should include events that offer youth opportunities to make significant faith decisions. But we can't stop there.

sanctifying grace

The final movement of God's grace is sanctifying grace. United Methodists understand salvation to be a process, not just a one-time event. Gradually, God transforms us into the persons whom God intends for us to be. This gradual transformation is called sanctification. Prayer, service to others, study and reflection, fellowship with the family of faith, worship, and many other spiritual practices empower us to grow and mature in our faith, so that we may be more like Jesus. Actions such as these are also evidence that we are aware of our union with God and our need to grow. Our programs and ministries for youth should help youth mature in perfect love, and they should vary in spiritual depth because youth are at different stages in their spiritual development.

TACKLING THE TOUGH QUESTIONS

This complex topic is difficult to cover in a single Confirmation lesson. And frankly, it's not a subject that is likely to enthrall most youth. Yet youth often have questions related to this topic. For example, a youth may want to know why your church does not do an altar call every week when at her friend's church or youth group such events happen frequently. Another youth may have heard that he will go to hell if he doesn't "pray the sinner's prayer." Questions may arise about whether persons in other faiths are saved or loved by God. To questions like these, Wesley's theology of grace provides a significant way of approaching the character and activity of God in the world.

As you explore this topic with youth, please remember the following:

- First, it is not your job to "convert" youth. Remember that grace is a gift of God.
- Second, youth should never be made to feel guilty if they have not accepted Christ's love for themselves or if they are unsure if they want to. The process of spiritual development is on the Holy Spirit's timetable, not yours.
- Finally, it is not the names of the three movements of grace that are critical for youth to know (although it's great when they do memorize them). Rather, youth need to hear that God is truly at work in them—and in their friends and family members—and will continue to be so throughout their lives.

SUPPLIES AND PREPARATION

BASIC SUPPLIES

- ☐ Bibles of various translations
- ☐ markerboard or large sheets of paper
- ☐ markers
- ☐ pens or pencils

- ☐ clear tape and/or glue
- ☐ masking tape
- ☐ index cards or paper cut about the same size (3-by-5 or 4-by-6)
- ☐ sheets of posterboard

- ☐ paper (Use paper that has already been used on one side as much as possible, depending on the activity.)
- ☐ scissors

ACTIVITY	PREPARATION	OTHER SUPPLIES
Opening Ritual	Write the meditation—adapted from Psalm 67—on a markerboard; or project the meditation, using the slide on the website.	☐ vine from previous sessions ☐ vine leaves (1 for each student)
Opener: Faith Walk	Plan the route for the walk. Have on hand extra adults.	☐ blindfolds, 1 for every 2 youth ☐ extra adult helpers
House of Salvation	Make copies of "House of Salvation" handout, from the website.	☐ copies of the "House of Salvation" handout
Prevenient Clays	Optional: Create your own sculpture as an example.	☐ copies of "House of Salvation" from the previous activity ☐ modeling clay ☐ tools for modeling the clay
Amazing, Justifying Grace	Gather supplies.	☐ hymnals or copies of the song "Amazing Grace"
Sanctifying Grace: An Object Lesson	Gather supplies.	☐ plastic bag full of water ☐ needle
Growing Toward Perfection (Optional)	Draw or create with paper a bare tree (with branches but no leaves) that is at least three feet tall. Make copies of the "Growth in Grace" handout from the website.	☐ drawn or created tree ☐ green paper ☐ leaf template or real leaves ☐ optional: note card ☐ copies of the "Growth in Grace"
Bible Study: What Kind of Grace?	Make copies of the "What Kind of Grace?" handout from the website.	☐ copies of the "What Kind of Grace?" handout
Closing Ritual	Write the benediction, "John Wesley's Rule," on a markerboard; or print out the poster from the website.	

OPTIONAL VIDEO

Way of Salvation	Preview the video.	☐ *Credo Confirmation Multimedia Teaching Tools* (the DVD) ☐ equipment with which to show the video

supplies
- vine from previous sessions
- vine leaves (1 for each student)
- markers or pens

preparation: Write the opening meditation—which is adapted from Psalm 67—on a markerboard; or project the meditation, using the slide on the website.

note: Take time before you get started to talk with the confirmands about what they read and wrote in the "New Creation" section of their CREDO STUDENT JOURNAL.

supplies
- blindfolds, enough for half of your group
- extra adult helpers

preparation: Think about the route that you will lead the youth through. (See the note in the margin on page 17.) Have on hand extra adults to act as spotters, as necessary.

opening ritual
(10 minutes)

As confirmands arrive, point them to your confirmation vine; and give each person a leaf. Invite the confirmands to reflect on the previous session and to write on their leaf something they learned or experienced during that session. Ask the confirmands to affix their leaf to the vine. Remind them that these leaves represent ways that we, as Christians and United Methodists, grow in our faith and more fully experience God's grace.

Then invite the youth to read aloud this opening meditation, adapted from **Psalm 67:**

> O God, be gracious to us and bless us
>   and make your face to shine upon us,
> that your way may be known upon earth,
>   your saving power among all nations.
> Let the peoples praise you, O God;
>   let all the peoples praise you!
> Let the nations be glad and sing for joy,
>   for you judge the people with equity
>   and guide the nations upon earth.

opener: faith walk (optional)
(10–15 minutes)

Have the confirmands pair off and decide which person in the pair will be a tour guide and which will be a tourist in an activity. (Don't tell them what you are planning to do.) Hand out blindfolds to the tourists, and have them sit down.

Say: "We are going to go for a walk together. Those of you who are blindfolded tourists will obviously not know where you are going, but you will be gently guided. Those of you who are tour guides, come with me."

Take the tour guides to a place out of earshot of the tourists, and explain the activity. Tell them that they are to guide the tourists as gently, as softly, and with as little direct (hands-on) interference as possible. They also should be very encouraging and not critical of the tourists. They may whisper or speak quietly to their tourist; and they may, when necessary, very gently guide with a touch of the hand, but they should not constantly talk to or touch their tourist. They should watch out for other pairs, and slow down or stop as necessary so that everyone has plenty of room. Everyone in the group must follow you on the journey.

Answer any questions the tour guides may have. Then allow the guides to go back to get their partners and follow you.

Guide the whole group. Additional adult leaders may be stationed throughout the group to observe and to give reminders as needed.

When you have reached your final destination, ask the tourists to leave their blindfolds on. Ask the tourists:

> ❧ Tourists, where do you think you are? (Let them make a few guesses.)

Have the tourists take their blindfolds off. Then ask them questions such as the following that will help them describe their experience:

> ❧ What did your tour guide do that helped you get to this place safely?

> ❧ What was unusual or surprising about how you were guided?

> ❧ Did you need more guidance, or did you get the right amount?

Ask the tour guides questions such as the following to describe their experience:

> ❧ What was it like trying to be quiet, gentle, and as hands-off as possible during this activity?

> ❧ If I hadn't given you instructions but had just told you to lead your partner however you wanted to, what, do you think, might you have done instead?

Say: "Today we're going to talk about the life of faith and how God's grace guides us every step of the way."

Then ask the whole group:

> ❧ How do you think this activity is like or unlike the way that God guides people?

VIDEO OPTION: WAY OF SALVATION
(5–10 minutes)

If you have a copy of *Credo Confirmation Multimedia Teaching Tools*, show the "Way of Salvation" video segment. This video is an overview of the three movements of God's grace and how we understand salvation as United Methodist Christians.

HOUSE OF SALVATION
(10 minutes)

Ask:

> ❧ What comes to mind when you hear the word *grace*?
> ❧ How would you define the word *grace*? (Possible definitions might include *"an undeserved gift," "a prayer given before a meal,"* or *"patience and forgiveness."*)

Then say: "For Christians, grace is the way we experience God's extraordinary love and forgiveness. God's grace allows us to feel God's presence and to understand what God is

NOTE: If you meet during a time when a lot of other classes or events are taking place, you may choose to map out a route for the youth to take. Choose or create a route that has some challenges (obstacles, a few stairs) but that will not put the youth in harm's way. The route should take about 10 minutes to complete at a slow pace. When planning this, be sensitive to and respectful of any physical limitations of members of your group. Plan ahead for the rest of your class session: Will you circle the group back during this activity, walk back after you're done, or hold the rest of the session at your destination?

Supplies
❏ *Credo Confirmation Multimedia Teaching Tools* (the DVD)
❏ equipment with which to show DVD videos

supplies
❑ markerboard
❑ marker
❑ copies of "House of Salvation" handout

preparation: Make copies of the "House of Salvation" handout from the website.

supplies
❑ Bible
❑ copies of "House of Salvation" handout from the previous activity
❑ modeling clay (at least a 1- by 2-inch chunk)
❑ tools for modeling with clay, such as craft sticks, butter knives, spoons

preparation:
Optional: Create your own sculpture as an example.

calling us to do. In the United Methodist tradition, we recognize three types, or movements, of grace: prevenient grace, justifying grace, and sanctifying grace."

Write each of these types of grace on a markerboard.

Hand each youth a copy of the "House of Salvation" handout from the website. Explain that John Wesley used the metaphor of a house to illustrate God's grace and salvation. Throughout this session, you'll refer to the house illustration.

PREVENIENT CLAYS
(10–15 minutes)

Say: "United Methodists believe that we experience God's grace throughout our lives, even before we are aware of God or have any idea what grace is. The grace that we experience before we are aware of it is called prevenient grace. *Prevenient* means 'going before.' Through prevenient grace, God seeks us out and invites us into a relationship. God's prevenient grace also helps us to make wise choices and discern the difference between good and evil."

Point to the "House of Salvation" handout.

Say: "John Wesley compared prevenient grace to the porch in front of the house. When we experience prevenient grace, God has invited us into the house; but we haven't yet accepted the invitation."

To further illustrate prevenient grace, hand out the clay and instruments for shaping it. Then read aloud **Isaiah 64:8.**

Give these instructions:

> I'd like for you to imagine that this clay is you and that God is the potter who shapes it.
>
> Think of a simple object that represents who you are. Use the tools to carve and/or mold the object from the clay, but carve or mold only on the left half. (It's OK for them to mold the right side, instead of the left, if they'd rather.)
>
> Without splitting the lump of clay in half, leave the other side alone so that it remains an unshaped block.
>
> The half you carve represents the ways that God's grace has already been active in your life. So if you choose, the object you sculpt may relate to your faith in some way. The other half represents the fact that God's grace will continue to work in your life in the future, in ways you can't now imagine."

Give the youth several minutes to work on their sculptures. Then regroup and allow volunteers to describe their sculptures to the rest of the group. Be particularly sensitive to the discussions, for youth might tell very personal stories.

AMAZING, JUSTIFYING GRACE
(15 minutes)

Hand out hymnals or copies of the song "Amazing Grace." Sing the song together or listen to a recording of the song.

Ask:

> ♣ What does the author of the song understand to be true about God's grace?

Make a list of their responses on a markerboard. Then ask:

> ♣ Have you ever heard your friends or some people of faith talk about being saved? What, do you think, did they mean by that phrase?

Return to the "House of Salvation" handout.

Say: "When we respond to God's invitation and open the door into God's house, we experience the second movement of God's grace: *justifying grace*. Justifying grace pardons our sins and makes us right with God. This is God's gift to us. God has acted in and through Jesus Christ, who made atonement for our sins, and that's the amazing grace we sang about earlier. We do not earn God's justifying grace. The choice we have is whether we will or will not respond to God's grace in faith and whether we will confess Jesus Christ as our Lord and Savior."

To help the confirmands remember the meaning of justifying grace, write the following on a markerboard:

> Justified
> Just-if-ied
> Just-if-I'd (as in "just [as] if I'd never sinned")

Ask:

> ♣ How can we respond to God's grace and accept God's invitation to live a new life? (Possible answers: *by repenting of our sins, by committing to spend time each day alone with God, by trying to do God's will in all situations, by leaving behind habits that have a negative effect on our relationship with God and others*.)
> ♣ How do our lives change when we experience God's justifying grace and know that God forgives all of our sins?

supplies
❏ hymnals or copies of the song "Amazing Grace"
❏ markerboard
❏ marker
❏ copies of the "House of Salvation" handout from previous activity

Credo Confirmation: Grace and the Way of Salvation

supplies

- ❏ plastic bag full of water
- ❏ needle
- ❏ copies of the "House of Salvation" handout from previous two activities
- ❏ tape

Sanctifying Grace: an Object Lesson

(10 minutes)

Refer again to the "House of Salvation" handout.

Say: "When we experience justifying grace, we enter the house. And once we're in the house, we find a lot of rooms for us to explore. The type of grace we experience after we have responded to God's invitation and been assured that our sins are forgiven is called *sanctifying grace*. To help you understand sanctifying grace, we're going to step away from the house metaphor and do a little demonstration."

Ask for two volunteers. Give the first volunteer a plastic bag full of water and the second volunteer a needle.

Say: "This bag of water represents you, filled with all of the talents and goodness and gifts that God has given you. This needle represents sin, those actions we do that interfere with our relationship with God and others."

Ask the volunteer with the needle to poke the bag of water, then ask the confirmand with the bag, "What has happened to you?"

Say: "Sin causes us to deflate a bit, and it prevents us from living the whole, full life that God intends for us. The good news is that God forgives us of our sin."

Use tape to cover the hole so that the bag doesn't leak. Then ask the person with the bag: "This tape represents God's forgiveness. Now, are you back to where you started?" (*No, you are still deflated.*)

Say: "The thing is, we need a way for our lives to be refilled and for grace to grow in our lives. That's what Wesley called sanctifying grace—God's grace that helps us grow throughout our entire life to be more like God."

Growing Toward Perfection (optional)

(10 minutes)

Say: "We've been creating a (vine/tree) as part of our Confirmation experience. Today, we're going to add another tree that will illustrate to the congregation the idea of sanctifying grace. We'll work together to draw icons on tree leaves for various ways that people can continue to grow in grace throughout their lives."

Set out green paper and (if you have them) leaf templates and ask the confirmands to trace and cut out leaves. While the youth are working, hand out copies of the "Growth in Grace" handout from the website.

Tell the confirmands to select an item from the "Growth in Grace" list, write it on a leaf, and draw a small picture on the leaf to represent that item. For example, a leaf that said,

"Worship each Sunday," might include a picture of a candle or an altar or the outside of a church sanctuary.

As the confirmands finish the leaves, have the youth use glue or tape to add the leaves to the tree. Allow confirmands to work on multiple leaves, and encourage the youth to work together to make sure that each of the items on the list is included on at least one leaf.

Then ask:

- ❧ Which of these practices of faith are you most familiar with? least familiar with?
- ❧ How do these practices help us grow closer to God and better do God's will?
- ❧ How, do you think, can we as a class help teach the rest of the congregation about sanctifying grace and these practices of faith?

For the last question, in particular, take some time to talk about their answers and to begin making some initial plans, as appropriate.

Optional: Place your tree where the entire congregation can see it. Ask a volunteer to write on a note card an explanation of the tree and what it represents.

Ask:

- ❧ Are any of you perfect?
- ❧ Is it possible for a human to be perfect? Explain.

Say: "John Wesley believed that Christians could reach perfection, or entire sanctification. Reaching Christian perfection does not mean that a person no longer sins, but it does mean that one is completely in tune with God's will and has complete faith that God can deliver him or her from sin."

BIBLE STUDY: WHAT KIND OF GRACE?
(15 minutes)

Hand out copies of the handout "What Kind of Grace?" to each youth, and divide the group into pairs or groups of three. (If you have five or fewer confirmands, have them work as one group.)

Say: "Now that you're getting to be experts on grace, let's see whether you can identify the kind of grace mentioned in some passages from the Bible. With your partner, look up the passages and write either *prevenient, justifying,* or *sanctifying* grace next to each verse."

Give the youth several minutes to work, and then go through their answers together. If there is disagreement on some of the Scriptures, ask the confirmands to talk about why they chose to call the item a certain type of grace. As needed, clarify the differences between prevenient, justifying, and sanctifying grace.

supplies
- ❏ drawn or created tree (See "preparation, below.)
- ❏ green paper
- ❏ leaf template to make leaves of the appropriate size for the tree (Or have the youth use real leaves as templates.)
- ❏ optional: note card
- ❏ pens or pencils
- ❏ scissors
- ❏ glue or tape
- ❏ copies of the "Growth in Grace" handout

preparation: Draw or create with paper a bare tree (with branches but no leaves) that is at least three feet tall. Make copies of the "Growth in Grace" handout from the website.

supplies
- ❏ Bibles
- ❏ copies of the "What Kind of Grace?" handout
- ❏ pens or pencils
- ❏ scissors
- ❏ glue or tape

preparation: Make copies of the "What Kind of Grace?" handout from the website.

NOTE: Before you dismiss, instruct the confirmands to read, reflect on, and journal about the material in the "Way of Salvation" section of the CREDO STUDENT JOURNAL before your next session. Also encourage them to try to do the activities related to "Way of Salvation" on the confirmand website.

supplies
- ❏ markerboard
- ❏ marker

preparation: Write the benediction, "John Wesley's Rule" (on page 22), on a markerboard; or print out the poster from the website.

CLOSING RITUAL
(10 minutes)

Gather the confirmands into a circle. Lead the youth in prayer, giving thanks to God for your time together and for all that the group has learned and experienced. Then go around the circle, inviting each person to pray aloud one word or phrase that describes something he or she learned during the past week of confirmation. After every person has had a chance to contribute a word or phrase, say a brief closing prayer, such as this one:

> God who goes before us, we're grateful to you for your action in our lives. God who moves us to moments of decision, we invite you to act anew in us today. God who will guide us throughout all of our lives, we promise to do our part to grow in faith. We're grateful for the fact that our salvation is a process, and that your grace will never leave us. Amen.

Then invite the confirmands to say aloud and in unison the benediction, "John Wesley's Rule."

Worship and Sacraments

INTRODUCTION

Regular worship with a community of faith is essential to being a follower of Christ and living a holy life. Worship is the most comprehensive way in which a congregation rehearses its faith and is recharged by God. In his three General Rules, John Wesley named worship as an "ordinance of God" that faithful Christians should attend to.

Worship is also where Christians gather to celebrate the two sacraments that were ordained by Jesus himself: baptism and Holy Communion.

WORSHIPING AS THE BODY OF CHRIST

When a community of believers worships together, each member of that community is accountable to every other member of the community. The members of the church support one another, strengthen one another, and grow together in holiness.

Young Christians who are considering confirming their faith and making a commitment to a life of discipleship need to get into the habit of worshiping each week with their congregation. John Wesley named many aspects of community worship—participating in sacraments, praying with the congregation, listening to sermons, and the reading of Scripture—as means of grace, ordinary ways in which God conveys grace to humankind. Participating in weekly worship opens young Christians to God's grace, allowing them to mature in faith.

A HOLY MYSTERY

Sacraments are not the only ways in which we receive God's grace, but they are unique in that they were ordained by Jesus himself. Jesus was baptized by John (**Mark 1:9**) and told his followers to go and baptize people "in the name of the Father and of the Son and of the Holy Spirit" (**Matthew 28:19**). And during his final meal with his disciples before his crucifixion, Jesus instituted the sacrament of Holy Communion, instructing his disciples to partake of his body and blood—the bread and cup—"in remembrance" of him (**1 Corinthians 11:23-26**).

Cleansed by the Waters of Baptism

Baptism is an initiation. It is the sacrament that draws us into the body of Christ as a member of the universal church, The United Methodist Church, and the local congregation. Baptism is an act of the Holy Spirit, and persons of any age can be baptized. Because we affirm God's prevenient grace—the grace by which God seeks us out and prepares us for faith—we often baptize infants and small children who are too young to take the baptismal vows for themselves. Their parents take the vows on their behalf.

Since baptism is an initiation into the church, the entire worshiping congregation participates in the sacrament. Members of the congregation reaffirm their faith and promise to support and nurture the person being baptized.

If they choose to be confirmed, some of your confirmands may be affirming the baptismal vows taken on their behalf when they were babies. Others may be receiving the sacrament of baptism during the confirmation service. In either case, they need to understand that baptism is a means of grace, and act of the Spirit, and an initiation into Christ's body, the church.

Nourished by the Lord's Supper

While a person may be baptized only once, Christians may and should partake frequently in the sacrament of Holy Communion. Through Communion, we are nourished by God's saving grace and reminded of the sacrifice Jesus made for our redemption.

As with baptism, the Holy Spirit is at work in Holy Communion. And, as with baptism, Holy Communion requires the participation of a community of faith. (Notice that *Communion* and *community* share a root word.) Celebrating Communion not only draws us closer to God, but also draws us closer to one another.

Different Style, Same Purpose

Congregations vary in their style of worship. Some worship in large, ornate sanctuaries with wooden pews and stained-glass windows; others worship in spaces rented from schools or community centers. Some sing classic hymns from a printed hymnal; others sing contemporary praise songs projected on a screen. Some celebrate Holy Communion each week; others celebrate the sacrament once a month.

We should celebrate this diversity of music and worship space. But young Christians need to understand that, regardless of the songs we sing or the architecture of the buildings where we gather, our worship should involve gathering, praise, the reading and proclaiming of Scripture, the affirmation of faith, prayers for the congregation and the world, thanksgiving, and a sending forth into the world to live as faithful disciples of Christ.

SUPPLIES AND PREPARATION

BASIC SUPPLIES

- ☐ Bibles of various translations
- ☐ markerboard or large sheets of paper
- ☐ markers
- ☐ pens or pencils

- ☐ clear tape and/or glue
- ☐ masking tape
- ☐ index cards or paper cut about the same size (3-by-5 or 4-by-6)
- ☐ sheets of posterboard

- ☐ paper (Use paper that has already been used on one side as much as possible, depending on the activity.)
- ☐ scissors

ACTIVITY	PREPARATION	OTHER SUPPLIES
Opening Ritual	Write the meditation—adapted from Psalm 67—on a markerboard; or project the meditation, using the slide on the website.	☐ vine from previous sessions ☐ vine leaves (1 for each student)
Worship Scavenger Hunt	Choose an option. If you choose Option B, gather appropriate supplies	☐ optional: supplies for Option B only
A Color for Every Season		☐ optional: church paraments
Question Ball	Inflate the ball or balloon, and write on it questions related to baptism and Holy Communion.	☐ beach ball or balloon ☐ permanent marker
What Is Baptism?	Gather supplies.	☐ copies of *The United Methodist Hymnal*
Babies and Believers		
Remember Your Baptism (Optional)	Prepare an altar setting.	☐ *The United Methodist Hymnal* ☐ pitcher filled with water ☐ basin ☐ small, smooth stones
What Is Holy Communion?	Gather supplies.	☐ copies of *The United Methodist Hymnal*
The Table Is Open		
You're in Charge	Choose an option. If you choose Option B, gather appropriate supplies.	☐ variety of worship bulletins ☐ copies of *The United Methodist Hymnal*
Closing Ritual	Write the benediction, "John Wesley's Rule," on a markerboard; or print out the poster from the website.	

OPTIONAL VIDEOS

Worship **Sacraments**	Preview the videos.	☐ *Credo Confirmation Multimedia Teaching Tools* (the DVD) ☐ equipment with which to show the videos

supplies

- ❑ vine from previous sessions
- ❑ vine leaves (1 for each student)
- ❑ markers or pens

preparation: Write the opening meditation—which is adapted from Psalm 67—on a markerboard; or project the meditation, using the slide on the website.

note: Take time before you get started to talk with the confirmands about what they read and wrote in the "Way of Salvation" section of their CREDO STUDENT JOURNALS.

supplies

- ❑ *Credo Confirmation Multimedia Teaching Tools* (the DVD)
- ❑ equipment with which to show DVD videos

opening ritual
(10 minutes)

As confirmands arrive, point them to your confirmation vine; and give each person a leaf. Invite the confirmands to reflect on the previous session and to write on their leaf something they learned or experienced during that session. Ask the confirmands to affix their leaf to the vine. Remind them that these leaves represent ways that we, as Christians and United Methodists, grow in our faith and more fully experience God's grace.

Then invite the youth to read aloud this opening meditation, adapted from **Psalm 67:**

> O God, be gracious to us and bless us
>   and make your face to shine upon us,
> that your way may be known upon earth,
>   your saving power among all nations.
> Let the peoples praise you, O God;
>   let all the peoples praise you!
> Let the nations be glad and sing for joy,
>   for you judge the people with equity
>   and guide the nations upon earth.

video option: worship
(5–10 minutes)

If you have a copy of *Credo Confirmation Multimedia Teaching Tools*, open this session with the "Worship" video segment. This video is an overview of why we worship, the pattern of Christian worship, and the seasons of the Christian calendar.

worship scavenger hunt
(15 minutes)

If your sanctuary or main worship space is available during class time, proceed to Option A and ignore Option B. If it is not available, skip Option A and continue with Option B. You may need to make some adjustments to this activity to reflect the layout of your worship space.

Option A
Take your class to the sanctuary, and gather in the center. Call out a word from the list below and have the confirmands identify the item by going to it and placing a hand on it.

Once the confirmands have correctly identified the item, ask them to define its purpose in worship. Read the item's corresponding paragraph.

Option B

1. Give the students a sheet of paper, and have them sketch the layout of a sanctuary inspired from a current or past church.
2. Instruct the students to include the following items in their drawings: altar, cross, pulpit, baptismal font, Communion rail. Have them add paraments later, after you discuss what paraments are. Make sure adults are available to assist youth who aren't familiar with some of these items.
3. Go over each item with the students. Ask the confirmands whether they know the purpose of each item. Before moving on to the next word, give the youth the information associated with each item, below.

Scavenger Hunt List for Both Options

- **Altar:** The Israelites used the altar as a place to give offerings to God. This included the best items someone might possess, such as crops from the harvest, precious metals, and even livestock. As Christians, we recognize that Christ has made the ultimate sacrifice and that God no longer desires these items as a sacrifice. Instead, we offer the one thing to God that is desired most, our heart. Today, the altar continues to represent the grace Christ offers through the sacrament of Holy Communion.

- **Cross** (or other symbols)**:** The cross is one of many symbols in the Christian church. The empty cross is a reminder of Christ's resurrection and victory over sin and death. Many church sanctuaries also use fire to symbolize another person of the Trinity, the Holy Spirit. In many congregations, acolytes bring in the light at the beginning of a worship service to light candles that burn throughout the service. Some churches have a perpetual light, a light that hangs in the corner of the sanctuary and is continually lit. It also reminds us that the Holy Spirit is constantly with us.

- **Pulpit:** The pulpit is where the pastor addresses the congregation and (in many churches) delivers the sermon. In many sanctuaries, a similar structure, called a lectern, stands on the opposite side of the chancel (front of the sanctuary). Lay persons stand at the lectern when they read Scripture or lead responsive readings.

- **Baptismal Font:** This is the basin of water used in baptism. United Methodists affirm baptism by affusion (pouring) and immersion. However, most United Methodist baptisms are done by aspersion (sprinkling), because of its gentleness to infants and its simplicity in worship. Churches that baptize by immersion, such as Baptist churches, often have a baptismal pool in the sanctuary.

- **Communion Rail:** Kneeling before the Lord as we celebrate the sacrament of Holy Communion shows humility and honors God.

Supplies for Option b
- ❏ paper
- ❏ pens or pencils

Preparation: Option A requires no supplies, just access to the sanctuary. Option B requires copies of a download from the website of a sanctuary layout or paper and pens and pencils for students to draw a sanctuary.

> **Paraments:** The seasons of the Christian calendar year, or liturgical year, each have a corresponding color, or colors. The colors in the sanctuary remind us of what we are celebrating and observing in worship.

a color for every season
(10 minutes)

Building on your discussion of paraments from the previous activity, say: "The colors of paraments and other sanctuary decorations correspond to the different seasons of the Christian calendar, or liturgical year. These seasons tell the story of our faith year after year and help us structure our worship services."

Ask the youth to name some seasons of the Christian year. Offer help as needed and work together until you've talked about each of the following seasons and the meaning behind each of these seasons. Show the paraments for each season as you discuss them if you have brought in paraments.

> **Advent:** a season of preparation for Christ's promised coming. Advent begins on the fourth Sunday before Christmas.

> **Christmas:** celebrates Jesus' birth. This season lasts from Christmas Eve until January 5, the day before Epiphany.

> **The Season After Epiphany:** celebrates Christ's divinity (frankincense), royalty (gold), and sacrifice (myrrh—used for anointing and embalming). This season begins on Epiphany, January 6, and continues until the Tuesday before Ash Wednesday.

> **Lent:** recalls Jesus' 40-day temptation in the wilderness and journey toward Jerusalem and the cross. The 40 days (not including Sundays) of Lent begin with Ash Wednesday and continue through Holy Week.

> **Easter:** celebrates Christ's resurrection. The Easter season goes from Easter Sunday until Pentecost.

> **Pentecost:** commemorates the outpouring of the Holy Spirit and the establishment of the church. Pentecost is the fiftieth day after Easter.

> **Ordinary Time:** a time to reflect on doing the work of God's kingdom and growing spiritually.

Name each of these seasons, and ask the confirmands to guess which color (or colors) the church associates with it. Answers and descriptions are below.

> **Advent:** Purple or blue (*Purple is the color of royalty, as we prepare for the coming of Jesus the King. Some churches today use blue to separate Advent from Lent, which also uses purple. Blue is the color of pre-dawn light.*)

- **Christmas:** White or gold (*These colors together signify a celebration, reserved for only the most important Christian holidays. These colors are also used on Epiphany, the day marking the arrival of the three wise men, typically celebrated on the first Sunday of January but, technically, January 6 each year.*)

- **Season After Epiphany:** Green (*Green is the color of growth, as we study the life of Jesus from child to man.*)

- **Lent:** Purple (*Purple is also the color of penitence.*)

- **Easter:** White or gold (*Like Christmas, this is one of the holiest and most celebrated days of the Christian year, Christ's resurrection.*)

- **Pentecost:** Red (*Red is the color of fire, which represents the Holy Spirit. Red may also be used in evangelistic or other services special to Christ's church, such as ordination.*)

- **Ordinary Time** (the time between Pentecost and Advent)**:** Green (*Green is the color of growth and symbolizes our growth in faith and understanding in the general teachings of Christ.*)

- **Communion** and **baptism** are not seasons, but they are represented by what color? White (*These sacraments signify the cleansing of the soul, through the grace of Jesus Christ.*)

video option: sacraments
(5–10 minutes)

If you have a copy of *Credo Confirmation Multimedia Teaching Tools,* show the "Sacraments" video segment. This video defines the sacraments and gives an overview of how United Methodists celebrate baptism and Holy Communion.

question ball (optional)
(5 minutes)

Say: "In worship we experience God's grace in many ways: through prayer, reading Scripture, passing the peace, listening to sermons, singing songs of praise, and so on. We also celebrate two rituals that were ordained by Jesus himself. In baptism and Holy Communion, God's grace is presence with us in a unique way."

Inflate a beach ball or balloon. Then use a permanent marker to write on the beach ball or balloon these questions (or others related to baptism and Holy Communion):

- How would you describe baptism to a friend who has never heard of baptism?
- How would you describe Communion to a friend who has never heard of it?

supplies
- [ ] *Credo Confirmation Multimedia Teaching Tools* (the DVD)
- [ ] equipment with which to show DVD videos

supplies
❑ beach ball or balloon
❑ permanent marker

preparation: Inflate the ball or balloon, and write on it questions related to baptism and Holy Communion.

> ❧ How is baptism in our church different from baptism in some of the churches your friends attend?
> ❧ How is Communion in our church different from Communion in some of the churches your friends attend?
> ❧ Who may be baptized in our church?
> ❧ Who may take Holy Communion in our church?
> ❧ What is one question that you have about baptism?
> ❧ What is one question that you have about Holy Communion?

Throw the ball to a confirmand. Ask him or her to read aloud the question under his or her left thumb and to answer it or open the question to the rest of the group. As needed, add information about the sacraments (such as the information on pages 51—52). Then have the confirmand with the ball pass the ball to another person, and ask this person to read aloud the question under his or her thumb. Continue until you've had a chance to discuss most of the questions. It is OK if some questions are repeated.

WHAT IS BAPTISM?
(5 minutes)

supplies
❑ copies of *The United Methodist Hymnal*

Hand out copies of *The United Methodist Hymnal* and ask the confirmands to turn to page 33, "The Baptismal Covenant I." Read through the baptismal service together, making note of the instructions for the pastor, which are in red. After you've read through the service, ask:

> ❧ What vows are being taken (or what promises are being made) in this baptismal service?
> ❧ Who is taking these vows? (*the person being baptized or those taking the vows on his or her behalf; the congregation*)

Point out that the vows of baptism are identical to the vows of confirmation (which the confirmands will learn about in detail in the next unit, "Live Your Commitment"). Also talk about the role of the congregation in baptism, and how the congregation vows to nurture one another and the person being baptized.

BABIES AND BELIEVERS
(10 minutes)

Say: "In The United Methodist Church, we baptize people of all ages. For infants and small children, who are unable to answer for themselves, parents or sponsors take the baptismal vows on their behalf."

Invite the confirmands to talk about whether they were baptized as infants or small children (even if they were baptized in another congregation or denomination) or have not been baptized and are considering being baptized during the confirmation service. Also invite them to talk about how they were baptized. (Was water gently applied to their head?

Were they fully immersed?) Assure them that all of these expressions of baptism are equally valid.

Ask:

❧ Why, do you think, do we baptize infants and small children in The United Methodist Church?

Explain that baptism is a sign of God's grace and that God's grace is at work in a person's life even before that person responds to God's grace by professing his or her faith. This is an example of the prevenient grace that confirmands learned about in the "Grace and the Way of Salvation" session. Also point out that infants and children in the church experience God's prevenient grace through the members of the congregation who have vowed to support, nurture, and teach them. Thus infant baptism involves the entire congregation.

Then say: "Not all Christian traditions baptize infants. Some practice what is called 'believer's baptism,' meaning that a person can be baptized only when he or she is old enough to make a person faith commitment. They believe that baptism before a person comes to faith is invalid."

Note that, along with The United Methodist Church, the Roman Catholic, Eastern Orthodox, Anglican (Episcopal in the U.S.), Lutheran, and Presbyterian churches and the United Church of Christ baptize infants. Baptists, Anabaptists (including Mennonites and the Amish), and Churches of Christ practice believer's baptism.

remember your baptism (optional)
(15 minutes)

Say a prayer of blessing over the water. For guidance, refer to "The Baptismal Covenant IV: Congregational Reaffirmation of the Baptismal Covenant" (pages 50–53, *The United Methodist Hymnal*).

Then remind those in the group who were baptized that, upon baptism, they received a new name—the name of Christ. Baptism is the formal entry into the body of Christ, the church. Then pour the water into the basin.

Invite participants who have been baptized to come to the basin and touch the water. As each person touches the water, make the sign of the cross in water on his or her forehead (much like you would make the sign of the cross in ashes on Ash Wednesday); and say to him or her, "Remember your baptism and be thankful."

Invite each person to take a small stone, marble, or bead from the basin as a reminder of their reaffirmation and remembrance of baptism.

Invite participants who have not yet been baptized to also come forward to receive a blessing in anticipation of their baptism. Say to these persons, "Anticipate your baptism and be thankful."

supplies
❏ copy of *The United Methodist Hymnal*
❏ pitcher filled with water
❏ basin
❏ small, smooth stones or large glass beads, marbles, or Lucite drops (available in arts and crafts stores, on the Internet, and in the craft or candle section of most large discount stores)

preparation: Prepare an altar setting that includes a pitcher with water and a basin containing the stones.

Note: Be clear that this is not a service of baptism. It is a ritual and a blessing, but it is not a sacrament.

Option: If all of the participants have been baptized, and if they feel comfortable doing so, have them pair off and invite partners to make the sign of the cross on each other's foreheads, saying, "Remember your baptism and be thankful."

supplies

❏ copies of *The United Methodist Hymnal*
❏ Bibles

WHAT IS HOLY COMMUNION?
(10–15 minutes)

Hand out copies of *The United Methodist Hymnal* and ask the confirmands to turn to page 6, "A Service of Word and Table I." Read through the service of Holy Communion together, making note of the instructions for the pastor, which are in red. After you've read through the service, ask:

➤ What does this service tell us about Holy Communion and why we take it?
➤ In this service, what sorts of things do we do to prepare for Holy Communion? (*confess our sins, offer one another signs of peace and love, give thanks to God, and so on*)

Ask a volunteer to read aloud **1 Corinthians 11:23-26.** Then say: "Like baptism, Holy Communion is a sacrament that Jesus ordained as a way for us to experience God's grace."

Have volunteers read aloud **Matthew 26:17-30,** in which Jesus celebrates the Passover with his disciples.

Afterward, ask:

➤ What celebration brought Jesus' disciples together?
➤ What, do you think, does Jesus want us to remember when we take Holy Communion? (*the sacrifice he made on our behalf, the forgiveness God gives us through Christ, the covenant that God has made with us through Christ*)

THE TABLE IS OPEN
(10 minutes)

Ask:

➤ Who is allowed to take Holy Communion in The United Methodist Church?

Allow a minute or two for answers and discussion, then read aloud this statement from *The United Methodist Book of Worship:*

> All who intend to lead a Christian life, together with their children, are invited to receive the bread and cup. We have no tradition of refusing any who present themselves desiring to receive.

Say: "United Methodists have an open table, meaning that 'All who intend to lead a Christian life' are welcome to participate in the sacrament. Not all Christian churches have an open table. Some, such as Roman Catholic, Eastern Orthodox, and certain Lutheran churches, have a closed table. These denominations serve Communion to only those persons who share their understanding of Holy Communion or who have been confirmed in their denomination."

Ask the confirmands whether they have had experiences of attending church with a friend and not being allowed to take Communion.

To help the confirmands understand why Christians have different views about who may take Communion, ask a volunteer to read aloud **1 Corinthians 11:27-28.**

Then explain that many churches that practice closed Communion believe that being worthy to take Holy Communion means being in a right relationship with the church and/or sharing the church's understanding of Holy Communion. United Methodists invite "all who love [God], who earnestly repent of their sin, and seek to live in peace with one another" to take Communion. It is up to the individual to determine whether he or she is worthy.

YOU'RE IN CHARGE
(15 minutes)

Say, "Now that we've learned about the different parts of worship, the setting, and the reasons we worship, we're going to plan our own worship service."

Parts planned may be used in their confirmation worship service or used at some other appropriate time.

1. Give each student a worship bulletin as an example.
2. Write on a markerboard the four movements of a worship service: 1) Entrance or Gathering, 2) Proclamation & Response, 3) Thanksgiving and Communion, 4) Sending Forth.
3. Have students share as a group where they see all four movements in the worship services on their bulletins. There may be multiple answers to each movement.
4. Divide the students into pairs or small groups—4 groups, if possible. Assign each group one aspect of a worship service to work on. (If you have too few youth to divide into 4 groups, divide the youth into 2 groups; and have each group work on 2 aspects of the service. Or work as a class to plan all aspects of the service.) Suggested tasks are: write a call to worship, write an offertory prayer, pick hymns for the service, design a bulletin cover, write additional confirmation vows, and design worship paraments or other visuals for the altar.

supplies
- ❏ Bibles
- ❏ various copies of your church's worship bulletin and from other churches, if possible
- ❏ pens or pencils
- ❏ paper
- ❏ markerboard
- ❏ marker
- ❏ copies of *The United Methodist Hymnal*

preparation: Collect worship bulletins from your local church and other congregations. As much as possible, have a wide variety available. It is important to offer several examples of services.

NOTE: Before you dismiss, instruct the confirmands to read, reflect on, and journal about the material in the "Worship" and "Sacraments" sections of the CREDO STUDENT JOURNAL before your next session.

SUPPLIES
- ❑ markerboard
- ❑ marker

PREPARATION: Write the benediction, "John Wesley's Rule" (on page 22), on a markerboard; or print out the poster from the website.

CLOSING RITUAL
(5 minutes)

Gather the confirmands into a circle. Lead the youth in prayer, giving thanks to God for your time together and for all that the group has learned and experienced. Then go around the circle, inviting each person to pray aloud one word or phrase that describes something he or she learned during the past week of confirmation. After every person has had a chance to contribute a word or phrase, say a brief closing prayer, such as this one:

> God who goes before us, we're grateful to you for your action in our lives. God who moves us to moments of decision, we invite you to act anew in us today. God who will guide us throughout all of our lives, we promise to do our part to grow in faith. We're grateful for the fact that our salvation is a process, and that your grace will never leave us. Amen.

Then invite the confirmands to say aloud and in unison the benediction, "John Wesley's Rule."

Wesleyan Quadrilateral

INTRODUCTION

Let's face it: Youth are frequently not the best decision-makers. Lots of factors come into play here, factors such as hormones, social identity, inexperience, and the process of individuation (separating oneself from one's parents and taking on an individual identity). Additionally, brain research has shown that the frontal cortex of the brain—the logic center—essentially shuts down during much of the teenage years. So if a teenager has ever exasperated you by the choices he or she made, take heart; it will get better.

Youth can certainly learn ways to become better decision-makers, and one way to explore this with youth is to introduce (or re-introduce) them to a process called "discernment." Discernment is a process of prayer, study, and reflection for the purpose of clarifying one's path in life, making decisions, and knowing God's will. Through discernment, we begin to sort out those impulses and inclinations that simply arise from our own ego or other influences from the ones that come from. Discernment is also a process that is useful for a community of people as they strive together to be holy and to do God's will.

In this session, the youth will use a Wesleyan tool for discernment, the Quadrilateral. Although the term *quadrilateral* was not one used by John Wesley (the concept of the Wesleyan Quadrilateral was introduced by twentieth-century Methodist scholar Albert Outler), the elements of the Quadrilateral were certainly common in his writing. Wesley encouraged us to use Scripture, tradition, reason, and experience when making decisions and determining God's will for us today.

SCRIPTURE

By the time the youth reach their middle school years, many of them have figured out that Christians have a lot of differences of opinion, especially when it comes to the Bible. This session gives you a chance to talk briefly about what Scripture is and how we should read it.

For United Methodists, Scripture—as represented in the Old and New Testaments—is foundational to our process of discernment. Christians disagree tremendously at times on what Scripture is and how it should be read, understood, and applied. But Christians are universally in agreement that the

Bible is our foundational document, is important for our lives today, and (as stated in The Articles of Religion of The Methodist Church) contains "all things necessary to salvation."

Tradition

Early Christian writings and the authority of the Church of England had a profound influence on John Wesley and on his writing, as he was an Anglican pastor his entire life.

When we use tradition as a tool for discernment, we must look at all of Christian history, including more than two hundred years of United Methodist history, and consider how others have approached the issues we face today. While Scripture is our foundation, we cannot discount the witness of faithful Christians who have answered God's call in the centuries since the Old and New Testaments were written and compiled. We serve a living God who, in the person of the Holy Spirit, continues to work through individual Christians and through the church, teaching us how to respond faithfully to new issues and realities.

Experience

Wesley understood that our ideas are based on our experiences, but he had a particular interest in our religious experience. He believed that we could evaluate and learn from our experiences of God.

Unless we make note of the "God moments" in our lives, we're likely to forget them or to downplay their significance. Many youth have had significant moments of spiritual insight or occasions when they have felt God's presence in their lives. Other youth might not recall such experiences, but that doesn't mean that God was not present throughout the events of their life.

Young people need to understand that their individual experience is valuable, but they also must be aware of what they haven't experienced and how much they have to learn. They can benefit from the wisdom and perspectives of more seasoned Christians who can draw from a lifetime of experience.

Reason

Wesley felt that we are called by God to use our God-given rational abilities, but he also warned us against thinking that we can rely on reason alone. Our tradition is one in which we are allowed and encouraged to ask, "Does that make sense?" We may determine, for example, whether a particular position on a social issue is *reasonable*, that is, consistent with our understanding of the Bible, the teaching of the Christian church, and the best information we have from contemporary humanities and sciences. By using reason, we can "examine everything and hold on to what is good" (1 Thessalonians 5:21, CEB).

THE WORK OF DISCERNMENT

Discernment often requires careful listening to others, as well as a willingness to be moved toward a way of thinking and acting that is best for others and not just best for oneself. Individual congregations and entire denominations wrestle with many controversial topics. But despite these differences, we still can learn to value the other person, to respect the integrity of different points of view, and to move toward those positions that unite rather than divide us.

SUPPLIES AND PREPARATION

BASIC SUPPLIES

- ☐ Bibles of various translations
- ☐ markerboard or large sheets of paper
- ☐ markers
- ☐ pens or pencils

- ☐ clear tape and/or glue
- ☐ masking tape
- ☐ index cards or paper cut about the same size (3-by-5 or 4-by-6)
- ☐ sheets of posterboard

- ☐ paper (Use paper that has already been used on one side as much as possible, depending on the activity.)
- ☐ scissors

ACTIVITY	PREPARATION	OTHER SUPPLIES
Opening Ritual	Write the meditation—adapted from Psalm 67—on a markerboard; or project the meditation, using the slide on the website.	☐ vine from previous sessions ☐ vine leaves (1 for each student)
Introducing the Quadrilateral	Optional: Hang the wind chimes in the meeting space.	☐ wind chime with 3 chimes or a photo of one ☐ optional: a way to hang the wind chimes
Lectio Divina (Optional)		
Scripture as I See It	Make copies of the "Bible Statements" handout, from the website.	☐ copies of the "Bible Statements" handout
Scripture on Scripture	Make copies of the "Scripture on Scripture" handout, from the website.	☐ copies of the "Scripture on Scripture" handout
Tradition: Lingo	Make copies of the "UMC From *A* to *Z*" handout, from the website only.	☐ copies of the "UMC From *A* to *Z*" handout ☐ *The Book of Discipline*
Experiences of God		
Reason: We're in Agreement That . . .		
Putting It All Together	Make copies of the "Scenarios for Putting It All Together" handouts, from the website, making 1 copy of each handout for every 2 youth.	☐ copies of the "Scenarios for Putting It All Together" handouts
Making Holy Choices	Gather supplies.	☐ hat or bowl
Closing Ritual	Write the benediction, "John Wesley's Rule," on a markerboard; or print out the poster on the website.	

OPTIONAL VIDEO

Wesleyan Quadrilateral	Preview the video.	☐ *Credo Confirmation Multimedia Teaching Tools* (the DVD) ☐ equipment with which to show the video

Opening Ritual

(10 minutes)

As confirmands arrive, point them to your confirmation vine; and give each person a leaf. Invite the confirmands to reflect on the previous session and to write on their leaf something they learned or experienced during that session. Ask the confirmands to affix their leaf to the vine. Remind them that these leaves represent ways that we, as Christians and United Methodists, grow in our faith and more fully experience God's grace.

Then invite the youth to read aloud this opening meditation, adapted from **Psalm 67:**

> O God, be gracious to us and bless us
>   and make your face to shine upon us,
> that your way may be known upon earth,
>   your saving power among all nations.
> Let the peoples praise you, O God;
>   let all the peoples praise you!
> Let the nations be glad and sing for joy,
>   for you judge the people with equity
>   and guide the nations upon earth.

Video Option: Wesleyan Quadrilateral

(5–10 minutes)

If you have a copy of *Credo Confirmation Multimedia Teaching Tools,* open this session with the "Wesleyan Quadrilateral" video segment. This video gives an overview of each side of the Quadrilateral.

Introducing the Quadrilateral

(5–10 minutes)

Ask:

➤ What comes to mind when you hear the word *discernment*?

Say: "Discernment is a process of prayer, study, and reflection that helps us clarify our path in life, make decisions, and know God's will. It helps us know the difference between what *we* want and what *God* wants. And while discernment is important for personal decisions, it also is useful for a community of people as they seek together a way to live that is faithful to God."

Then say: "As United Methodists, we have a unique approach to making better decisions that is sometimes referred to as the *Quadrilateral,* which is a fancy word for a shape with four sides. We follow the advice of John Wesley to consider Scripture, tradition, experience, and reason when making decisions and trying to discern God's will for our lives. Today, we'll look at each of those four elements of decision-making."

supplies
- ❑ vine from previous sessions
- ❑ vine leaves (1 for each student)
- ❑ markers or pens

preparation: Write the opening meditation—which is adapted from Psalm 67—on a markerboard; or project the meditation, using the slide on the website.

note: Take time before you get started to talk with the confirmands about what they read and wrote in the "Worship" and "Sacraments" sections of their CREDO STUDENT JOURNAL.

supplies
- ❑ *Credo Confirmation Multimedia Teaching Tools* (the DVD)
- ❑ equipment with which to show DVD videos

supplies
- ❑ wind chime with 3 chimes or a picture of one
- ❑ optional: a way to hang the wind chimes

optional preparation: Hang the wind chimes in the meeting space.

Show the youth a wind chime—an actual one or a photo or drawing of one. Be sure to show a wind chime that has three chimes. (If you can bring in a wind chime, hang it from a doorway or window in the room before class.)

Ask:

❥ Suppose that the four parts of the Quadrilateral—Scripture, tradition, experience, and reason—are the parts of this wind chime. Which part of the Quadrilateral, do you think, would Wesley say is this part, the part that holds the chimes? Why?

After a short time for discussion, let the youth know that Wesley considered Scripture to be foundational and the "primary source and criterion for Christian doctrine and life." (This is why, in the Credo program, we often present the Quadrilateral as a trapezoid, with Scripture as the base and longest side.)

Ask:

❥ What else, do you think, is important about wind chimes that might help us understand how this is a good metaphor for the Quadrilateral? (*There may be many answers; but be sure to point out, if no one else does, that wind is an essential part. The wind, which in this metaphor represents the movement of the Holy Spirit within the community of faith, helps the wind chime ultimately fulfill its purpose: making music or, in our case, the "music" of theological reflection.*)

If you have a photo or drawing of wind chimes, label each of the parts according to the Quadrilateral.

Say, "Scripture, the Old and New Testaments, is where we as Christians look first when trying to discern what to do or think. Our tradition is our faith heritage, the history of God's continuing presence with followers of Christ. It includes the things the church has believed or done or said in the past. Experience refers to what we know to be true about God and the world from our own experience.

"We use our reasoning, or thinking, abilities to ask questions of faith, evaluate what we read in Scripture and what we learn from our tradition, and compare all of that with our experience."

LECTIO DIVINA (OPTIONAL)
(10 minutes)

Tell the youth that you're going to lead them in a Scripture-reading exercise called *Lectio Divina* (LEK-tee-oh dih-VEE-nah). Ask them to turn to **Luke 24:13-35,** or have them close their eyes and sit comfortably.

Explain that *Lectio Divina* is a meditative way of reading Scripture. You'll read the Scripture three times, with different instructions each time.

The first time, ask the confirmands to listen to the story and to pay special attention to any word or phrase that catches their interest. Read the passage slowly and with feeling.

supplies
❑ Bibles

Then ask the youth to call out the word or phrase that stood out for them. It is not critical that everyone respond.

Pause a short time; then tell the youth to listen to the story again and consider the question, "How does this Scripture touch my life?" Have one of the youth read the Scripture aloud. Then pause for a moment of silence while the class reflects.

Ask the youth to tell something about how the Scripture touched their life or how they heard God's voice in the passage. Again, it's not critical that every youth participate; but be sure to allow them the space and time to do so.

Have another youth read the Scripture aloud the third time. This time the youth should listen while keeping in mind the question, "What in this Scripture do I hear God inviting me to do or to change?"

Ask the youth to reflect on the question in silence for a minute. Then ask them to tell what invitation they heard in the Scripture.

End with a simple prayer.

scripture: as i see it
(10–15 minutes)

supplies
❑ copies of the "Bible Statements" handout

preparation: Make copies of the "Bible Statements" handout, from the website.

Say: "When it comes to the Bible, people have lots of different opinions about what it is, what is says, and what we're supposed to do with it. Let's think about where we stand right now on various questions about the Bible."

Point to 2 walls or chairs on opposite ends of the room, and explain that one side (*point to it*) represents "true," and the other side (*point to it*) represents "false." The youth should decide where along the spectrum they are—on one side or the other or somewhere in between.

Read the statements, one at a time, from the "Bible Statements" handout. After each statement, allow time for the youth to choose where they will stand. (Adult leaders—except the leader of this activity—may also participate.) Do not read the answers or the explanations at this point in the exercise.

Before reading the next statement, have a brief conversation with the youth about why they chose to stand where they did. Youth may, at any point, change their position and move to another point on the spectrum if they choose to do so.

After you have read each of the statements, have the youth take a seat. Give the youth a copy of the "Bible Statements" handout.

Have youth volunteers read aloud the statements and explanations. Notice that some of the items are definitively true or false, while others are more subjective.

supplies

❑ Bibles
❑ pens or pencils
❑ copies of the "Scripture on Scripture" handout

preparation: Make copies of the "Scripture on Scripture" handout, from the website.

supplies

❑ *The Book of Discipline*
❑ a markerboard or large sheet of paper
❑ markers
❑ pens or pencils
❑ copies of the "United Methodism From A to Z" handout

preparation: Make copies of the "United Methodism From A to Z" handout, from the website.

scripture on scripture

(10 minutes)

In this activity, we'll look at a few of the passages in the Bible that describe what Scripture is and that relate to the topic of discernment.

Distribute Bibles and copies of the "Scripture on Scripture" handout. Have the youth form small groups of 3–4 youth.

Ask the youth to read and talk briefly about all four of the passages, answering the questions on the handout. Give the groups about 6–7 minutes to work.

Tradition: Lingo

(10 minutes)

In this activity, you'll give the confirmands a chance to think of some words and phrases they associate with The United Methodist Church even if they do not completely understand their meanings.

Have the youth form small groups. Then hand out copies of "United Methodism From A to Z" one for each person or one for each group.

Say: "The United Methodist Church, like any denomination, has its own lingo that can sometimes seem strange to those who are not 'in the know.' I'm guessing that you might have added a few of these terms, names, acronyms, and so forth to your vocabulary. So work together to try to come up with at least one answer for each letter. When possible try to think of things that relate specifically to The United Methodist Church and not all churches." Pause for a moment to answer any questions.

Give the groups about 5 minutes to come up with ideas. Answers such as *God, salvation,* and *church* are good; but answers such as *General Conference, sanctifying grace,* and *cross and flame* are better examples of the lingo associated with United Methodism. Some letters will be difficult. (You might suggest *quadrennium*—the amount of time between General Conferences—for *Q*.) Be willing to accept names of persons from church history for especially tough letters. (You might suggest Andrew Zeller, an important early United Brethren bishop for *Z*.) For *X*, tell the confirmands that *X* resembles the Greek letter *chi*, which is the first letter in the Greek words for *Christ* and *Christian*.

It is OK if you don't come up with something for every letter. The point of the activity is that every religious tradition has its own language and uses this language to describe its beliefs and heritage.

Then ask:

❧ How can we know what The United Methodist Church says or believes about a certain subject?

Show the confirmands a copy of *The Book of Discipline*. Explain that every United Methodist Church is part of an annual conference. Annual conferences usually include all the United Methodist congregations in a state or region. Representatives from all the congregations in an annual conference gather once a year to vote on rules and recommendations for the churches in their area.

Then tell them that annual conferences send delegates to the General Conference, an event held every four years, in which delegates make decisions on behalf of the entire church.

Explain that the General Conference votes on all of the church's laws and procedures and that all of these rules and policies are published every four years in *The Book of Discipline*. *The Book of Discipline* also includes "Our Doctrinal Standards and General Rules"—which explains who we are and what we believe as United Methodist Christians—and the Social Principles—which are the stands that the church has taken on social, cultural, and political issues.

experiences of god
(10–15 minutes)

Ask the confirmands to name ways that people remember and keep track of their experiences. This might include filling photo albums, posting pictures on the Internet, writing in a journal, scrapbooking, keeping a video diary, and so forth.

Then ask:

❧ How do you remember and keep track of your experiences?
❧ Why, do you think, do people put so much effort into keeping track of memories and experiences?

Say: "Our experiences are important because they shape who we are, and because we can learn from them."

Invite the confirmands to spend a minute or two in silence, thinking about how they have experienced God. Perhaps they felt comfort during a tough time or felt someone nudging them to make the right decision. Maybe they felt God strengthening them when they faced temptation. Or maybe they felt God's presence in nature or in the love of another person.

After they've had time to reflect on how God has been present in their lives, divide the youth into pairs. Have the partners tell each other about their experiences of God. (They can be as specific or as vague as they would like.)

After about a minute, ask the partners to talk about what their experiences tell them about God. For example: "God watches over us and protects us," "God loves me," "God guides me and corrects me," "God gives me strength and courage," and so on.

Give the pairs plenty of time to discuss then invite them to talk about their experiences of God and what they learned about God from these experiences.

supplies
- markerboard
- marker
- large sheets of paper

reason: we're in agreement that . . .
(10–15 minutes)

Ask the youth to suggest topics that are highly controversial for young people, topics about which their friends often take opposite sides and have strong opinions. The topics may be serious, such as whether towns should have curfews for teens, or they may be silly, such as whether fish or gerbils make the best pets.

Write their suggestions—at least 6 of them—on a markerboard. Then ask the youth to narrow the list to one topic for every four or five confirmands. Have the confirmands break into groups of four or five, and assign each group a topic. (It is OK if you have only one group.)

Instruct the groups to write their topic across the top of a large sheet of paper. Ask the groups to divide into two teams, with teams taking opposite positions on their assigned topics. Give the teams about 2 minutes to prepare their arguments. Then ask the teams within each group to debate their topic. The only rule of the debate is to have fun.

After about 3 minutes of debate, stop the conversations (or arguments) and tell the teams that they need to switch gears. They now should determine what they can both agree on, using their reasoning skills to create a unified "position statement" on the issue being discussed. Have the unified groups write their statement of agreement on their large sheet of paper.

Discuss with the confirmands about the process they used and how this is good process that a group of church members or Christian groups could use when they have disagreements.

Ask:

- What role does our faith play when it comes to controversial topics?
- How does focusing on what we agree on move us forward and help us discuss the things we don't agree on?

putting it all together
(10 minutes)

Say: "Now that we've had a chance to explore all four parts of the Quadrilateral, we're going to try applying them to a real-life scenario. Before we do that, let's review just a bit." Ask:

- What are the four parts of the Quadrilateral? (*Scripture, tradition, experience, reason*)

❯ To what does each part refer? (**Scripture** *refers to the fact that our first, foundational resource in discernment is the Bible. Our* **tradition** *is the historic church and what Christians have done and believed throughout the ages. Our* **experience** *refers to our own experiences of faith and the depth of experience we've had in our own life.* **Reason** *is our ability to think through rationally all of these and to come to a decision that is reasonable.*)

Divide the youth into 2 groups, and give each group one of the scenarios on the website. You may choose to have all of the groups do the same scenario, or split the scenarios between several groups.

Ask the youth to read their group's scenario and then use Scripture, tradition, experience, and reason to discern a good course of action. Provide concordances, Bible dictionaries, or access to online Bibles and copies of *The Book of Discipline* and/or *The Social Principles* as available.

Allow the youth several minutes to work together, and then have them come back together as a group.

Read aloud, one by one, each of the scenarios, then have those who worked on it discuss what they concluded to be a good course of action.

MAKING HOLY CHOICES
(10–15 minutes)

Say: "Holiness has always been an important part of our United Methodist tradition. The first Methodists devoted themselves to 'going on toward perfection' by striving to do everything according to God's will. In addition to the Quadrilateral, John Wesley had three General Rules for the early Methodists who met in class meetings: Do no harm; do good; and attend to the ordinances of God. The 'ordinances of God' are practices of faith through worship, prayer, reading the Bible, and celebrating Holy Communion. Still today, these rules give us guidance for living a holy life."

Write these three rules on a markerboard.

Hand out scrap paper and pens or pencils. Have each person think of a difficult choice a teenager might have to make. (Examples might include: *choosing between going to church on Sunday or playing in a softball tournament or choosing whether or not to go to a party where there will be alcohol.*) Give the youth a few minutes to come up with their situations and then fold the papers. Then collect the folded papers in a hat or bowl.

Have the confirmands, one at a time, draw from the container and read aloud the situation. Have the class discuss the most holy response to each situation. Encourage the youth to consider Wesley's General Rules and the Wesleyan Quadrilateral.

supplies
☐ copies of the "Scenarios for Putting It All Together" handouts

preparation: Make copies of the "Scenarios for Putting It All Together" handouts, from the website, making 1 copy of each handout for every 2 youth.

supplies
☐ markerboard
☐ marker
☐ scrap paper
☐ pens or pencils
☐ hat or bowl

NOTE: Before you dismiss, instruct the confirmands to read, reflect on, and journal about the material in the "Wesleyan Quadrilateral" and "Living a Holy Life" sections of the CREDO STUDENT JOURNAL before your next session.

SUPPLIES
❑ markerboard
❑ marker

PREPARATION: Write the benediction, "John Wesley's Rule" (on page 22), on a markerboard; or print out the poster from the website.

CLOSING RITUAL
(10 minutes)

Gather the confirmands into a circle. Lead the youth in prayer, giving thanks to God for your time together and for all that the group has learned and experienced. Then go around the circle, inviting each person to pray aloud one word or phrase that describes something he or she learned during the past week of confirmation. After every person has had a chance to contribute a word or phrase, say a brief closing prayer, such as this one:

> God who goes before us, we're grateful to you for your action in our lives. God who moves us to moments of decision, we invite you to act anew in us today. God who will guide us throughout all of our lives, we promise to do our part to grow in faith. We're grateful for the fact that our salvation is a process, and that your grace will never leave us. Amen.

Then invite the confirmands to say aloud and in unison the benediction, "John Wesley's Rule."

Renounce, Accept, Confess

INTRODUCTION

"Do you renounce the spiritual forces of wickedness, reject the evil powers of this world, and repent of your sin?"

"Do you accept the freedom and power God gives you to resist evil, injustice, and oppression in whatever forms they present themselves?"

"Do you confess Jesus Christ as your Savior, put your whole trust in his grace, and promise to serve him as your Lord in union with the church, which Christ has opened to people of all ages, nations, and races?"

These statements, from "Baptismal Covenant I" in *The United Methodist Hymnal* (page 34), are the first vows your confirmands will make if they choose to be confirmed. A person who takes these vows indicates that he or she is making a commitment to a new way of life. He or she promises to reject wickedness, to embrace God's freedom to resist and turn away from sin and evil, to confess Christ as his or her Savior, and to be one with Christ's church. These vows should not be taken lightly.

renounce, reject, repent

Before one accepts God's freedom and confesses Christ, one must reject those things that disrupt one's relationship with God and others.

While words such as *evil* and *wickedness* certainly aren't new to confirmands, some younger adolescents might not recognize how these forces are at work in the world around them. It is easy to see evil in a heartless villain in a book or movie, but how is evil at work in our world, our communities, and our hearts? Once we identify these evil and wicked forces, how do we reject and renounce them? And what does it mean to repent of our sin?

By vowing to "renounce the spiritual forces of wickedness," confirmands are not vowing to be superheroes. Rejecting evil requires that they have an awareness of the ways in which sin and wickedness are at work in their lives and in the world around them. Confirmands must move beyond an understanding of evil as it is expressed in videogames and scary movies to the very real ways in which evil is at work in our world today. Rejecting evil also involves developing habits that bring them closer to God, God's will, and God's priorities.

accept

God offers us the freedom to resist evil and repent of sin. As expressed in the Articles of Religion of the Methodist Church, "God's initiative in salvation allows for, empowers, and requires a free human response to God's 'amazing grace'" (Article 8). But how will we accept this freedom? Will we use these abilities and opportunities to resist, cooperate with, or ignore "evil, injustice, and oppression in whatever forms they present themselves"?

What good news for young people! Freedom! In our United Methodist tradition, we understand that free will is most fulfilling when we temper it with discipline and accountability. Using our freedom in Christ, without being shaped, trained, or nurtured by spiritual discipline, is like being a gifted athlete who demonstrates exceptional strength, speed, and agility but doesn't know how to use his or her gifts to benefit the team and, therefore, struggles with the pressures of competition. For Christians, using one's free will without the training, practice, and accountability that come from spiritual disciplines and a Christian community often results in self-centered pursuits that do not bear fruit.

confess

Having repented of sin and accepted God's freedom, those taking these vows can confess Christ and their reliance on God's grace and promise to join with others in doing the work of God's kingdom. This confession is the culmination of our previous rejection of wickedness, evil, and sin and of acceptance of God's power to resist the same. This confession also identifies us as followers of Christ who have a responsibility to live our lives according to Jesus' teaching and faithfully represent Christ's holy church.

The final phrase in this vow of confession mentions Christ's holy church. By confessing Jesus, we join with "people of all ages, nations, and races." This echoes Paul's teaching in **Galatians 3:26-29:**

> For in Christ Jesus you are all children of God through faith. As many of you as were baptized into Christ have clothed yourselves with Christ. There is no longer Jew or Greek, there is no longer slave or free, there is no longer male and female; for all of you are one in Christ Jesus. And if you belong to Christ, then you are Abraham's offspring, heirs according to the promise.

SUPPLIES AND PREPARATION

BASIC SUPPLIES

- ❑ Bibles of various translations
- ❑ markerboard or large sheets of paper
- ❑ markers
- ❑ pens or pencils

- ❑ clear tape and/or glue
- ❑ masking tape
- ❑ index cards or paper cut about the same size (3-by-5 or 4-by-6)
- ❑ sheets of posterboard

- ❑ paper (Use paper that has already been used on one side as much as possible, depending on the activity.)
- ❑ scissors

ACTIVITY	PREPARATION	OTHER SUPPLIES
Opening Ritual	Write the meditation—adapted from Psalm 101:1-4—on a markerboard.	❑ vine from previous sessions ❑ vine fruit (1 for each student)
Promises, Promises	Gather supplies.	❑ wedding photo
Hear Evil, See Evil, Do Evil?	If you choose to use printouts of the home page of various Internet news sites, print them and make copies if you choose to.	❑ newspapers, news magazines, and/or printouts from various Internet news sites ❑ optional: Internet access and a way to project the screen
Totally Rejected	Make copies of the "D-Fining Words" and "General Rules" handouts.	❑ copies of the "D-Fining Words" and "General Rules" handouts
Turn Your Life Around	Gather supplies.	❑ copies of *The United Methodist Hymnal*
Freedom Rules!	Make copies of the "General Rules" handout, from the website.	❑ copies of *UM Hymnal* ❑ "General Rules" handout ❑ large sheets of paper or posterboard and art supplies
Transformers (Optional)	Make copies of the "Transformers: Christians Who Chose to Change the World" handout. Write on a markerboard the questions in the activity.	❑ copies of the "Transformers" handout
Signed, Sealed, Delivered		
Trust: The One Who Knows	Optional: Make copies of the "Confirmation Vows" handout, from the website.	❑ copies of *The United Methodist Hymnal* or of the "Confirmation Vows" worksheet
Closing Ritual	Write the benediction, "John Wesley's Rule," on a markerboard; or print out the poster on the website.	

OPTIONAL VIDEOS

Renounce, Reject, Repent Accept Confess	Preview the videos.	❑ *Credo Confirmation Multimedia Teaching Tools* (the DVD) ❑ equipment with which to show the videos

opening ritual
(10 minutes)

During the first unit, "Know Your Story," your confirmands added branches to a vine (or tree trunk) as part of a ritual inspired by **John 15:1-9.** During the second unit, "Confirm Your Faith," they added leaves to the branches. During this unit, "Live Your Commitment," the confirmands will be adding fruit. More information is available on the website.

As the confirmands arrive, give each person a cutout of a piece of fruit. Invite each person to write on his or her fruit cutout something that he or she learned, gained, or experienced during the "Confirm Your Faith" unit. Instruct the confirmands to attach their fruit to the branches.

Say: "Jesus says that, if we abide in him, we will 'bear much fruit' (**John 15:5**). For Christians, bearing fruit means living our lives according to God's will and doing God's work in the world. In this unit, we'll get a taste of some of these fruits, as we take a close look at our confirmation vows."

When all of the confirmands have arrived, invite each person to talk briefly about what he or she wrote on his or her piece of fruit. (You might also ask why he or she attached the fruit to a particular branch or near a particular leaf.) Then invite the youth to participate in the following responsive reading, adapted from **Psalm 101:1-4,** that you wrote on a markerboard beforehand:

Leader: We light this candle, remembering that Jesus is the light of the world.

We will sing to you, Lord! We will celebrate your kindness and your justice.

People: We will have nothing to do with evil.

Leader: Please help us learn to do the right thing, and we will be honest and fair in all we do.

People: We will have nothing to do with evil.

Leader: We refuse to be corrupt or to take part in anything crooked; we won't be dishonest or deceitful.

People: We will have nothing to do with evil.

Then hand out copies of *The United Methodist Hymnal,* and ask the confirmands to turn to the "Affirmation From 1 Corinthians 15:1-6 and Colossians 1:15-20" (888). Invite a volunteer to read the Leader part. Everyone else should read the part of the People.

promises, promises
(10 minutes)

supplies
- ❑ wedding photo of a couple (from your wedding album, from your friends or family, from a newspaper or an online wedding announcement)

Hold up the wedding picture for the students to see, then pass it around.

Ask:

- ❦ Why, do you think, am I showing you a wedding picture during a confirmation lesson?
- ❦ What do a wedding and a confirmation service (that is, a worship service in which people are confirmed) have in common? (*Both are religious services; both often take place in a church; a pastor usually presides over both; participants of both often dress up; family and friends are present at both; both have been prepared for and rehearsed; often both are followed by a reception; both involve taking vows.*)
- ❦ What vows, or promises, do couples make when they get married?
- ❦ Why are vows an important part of a wedding ceremony?

Following your discussion of vows and of the similarities between weddings and confirmation services, tell the confirmands that this unit will focus on the vows that they will have an opportunity to take during the confirmation worship service at the conclusion of your confirmation program. Make the following points:

- ❦ Just like a wedding, a service of confirmation involves vows. And, as with wedding vows, these vows must not be taken lightly. Confirmation vows are very special promises that those being confirmed make to God and to God's people, particularly those people who make up our particular faith community or local church.
- ❦ The sessions in this final unit of the CREDO confirmation program will prepare your confirmands to make these vows. It will be each student's choice whether or not to be confirmed. The purpose of the sessions in this unit is to help the confirmands make an informed decision by teaching them what these vows mean and how they will be expected to fulfill these vows.
- ❦ When a couple exchanges wedding vows (again hold up the wedding picture), the two persons are making promises to each other as they begin life together in a new relationship. If two people were to get married then say, "See ya," and went their separate ways, they obviously would not be keeping their vows. Similarly, when one is confirmed, that person enters into a new relationship with the church, a relationship marked by the vows that person makes in the presence of God and the church family.

video option: renounce, reject, repent
(5–10 minutes)

If you have a copy of *Credo Confirmation Multimedia Teaching Tools*, open this session with the "Renounce, Reject, Repent" video segment. This video introduces the first confirmation vow.

hear evil, see evil, do evil?
(10 minutes)

Hand out copies of *The United Methodist Hymnal* and read aloud the first confirmation vow from page 34:

On behalf of the whole church, I ask you:

Do you renounce the spiritual forces of wickedness,
    reject the evil powers of this world,
    and repent of your sin?

Ask:

❧ What words, phrases, or images come to mind when you hear the words *wickedness* and *evil*?
❧ What feelings do you connect with these words?
❧ What actions and events come to mind when you hear the words *evil* and *wickedness*? (You might choose to add examples such as *terrorism, slavery, genocide,* and *pollution* if the confirmands do not name them.)

Say: "Sometimes when we hear words like *evil* or *wicked*, we think of villains and situations from movies, books, or videogames."

Ask:

❧ What are some fictional persons or situations that you would describe as evil or wicked?

Then say: "Sadly, evil and wickedness aren't confined to imaginary worlds but are a very real part of our world."

If you have Internet access in your meeting space, go to a news website. (If possible, project the computer screen so that everyone can see it well.) Scroll through the headlines and ask the youth to point out news stories where they see examples of wickedness and evil. If you do not have Internet access, bring in copies of newspapers and news magazines or print outs of the homepages of assorted news websites.

After the confirmands have selected several examples, ask:

❧ What makes the events and/or people in these stories wicked or evil?

Then say: "Unfortunately, some of us—or our friends and family—have experienced evil in very up-close-and-personal ways, through forces such as violence, abuse, and addiction. Wickedness and evil don't just happen in faraway places. They touch people's lives and become very real to us and to people we care about."

Ask:

> ❧ Where do you see wickedness and evil in our community? in your school?
> ❧ How can wickedness and evil affect families and/or churches?

TOTALLY rejecteD
(10 minutes)

To help the confirmands better understand evil and wickedness, raise the following points:

> ❧ **Christians affirm that evil and wickedness are present in the world.** (You've named several examples already in this session.) But Christians also believe that God is always present and active and is more powerful than evil.
> ❧ **Evil is the result of sin.** Because all people are sinful, we create structures and institutions that exploit individuals and groups, create and sustain poverty, and destroy God's creation. Rejecting evil involves both resisting the temptation to do evil and resisting the temptation to encourage or participate in evil. That is, we should strive to eliminate sin in our lives and we should also be careful not to support groups and institutions that are responsible for evil on a larger scale.
> ❧ **Obviously, we are not God, and we have trouble seeing the big picture.** We see poverty, starvation, terrorism, abuse, and murder; and we become overwhelmed. It's tempting to say, "I'm too young to do anything about all this stuff." Sometimes, we even feel powerless to address evil in our homes and schools.
> ❧ **Our United Methodist tradition, and specifically our confirmation vows, give us some help in responding to the forces of evil and wickedness.**

Ask:

> ❧ Think back to the news stories involving evil and wickedness that we identified earlier. How were the people you read about in these stories rejecting evil?
> ❧ Whom have you known, or known of, who has taken a stand against evil? Who were they, and what did they do?

Then distribute copies of the "General Rules" handouts from the website.

Say: "When John Wesley was organizing Methodist groups in England in the eighteenth century, one of his rules for the early Methodists was to avoid 'evil of every kind.' He gave specific examples of the evil that we should avoid."

Ask volunteers to read aloud John Wesley's first General Rule for Methodist Societies, "Do No Harm," focusing on the examples

supplies
❏ copies of the "General Rules" handouts (only on the website)
❏ markerboard
❏ marker
❏ paper
❏ pens or pencils

preparation: Make copies of the "General Rules" handouts.

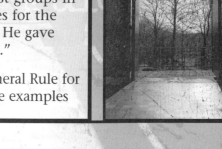

of evil that Wesley lists. Then challenge the confirmands to think about what examples of evil Wesley might list if he were writing today. Which items would remain unchanged, which would need to be revised or replaced, and what would need to be added? Record their ideas on a markerboard.

As time permits, ask the group to come to a consensus on a list of 10–15 items. Have a volunteer record these examples of doing harm on a sheet of paper. Ask another volunteer to take the list and to take responsibility for typing up the group's version of John Wesley's first rule, sending it to you so that you can send the document to the rest of the group, post it to a group page on a social networking site, or send it to someone who can post it on the congregation's website.

supplies
❏ copies of *The United Methodist Hymnal*
❏ paper
❏ pens or pencils

Turn Your Life Around
(5 minutes)

Take another look at the first confirmation vow:

> On behalf of the whole church, I ask you:
>
> Do you reject the spiritual forces of wickedness, reject the evil powers of this world, and repent of your sin?

Ask:

> ❧ In addition to *renounce* and *reject,* what is the third "r" word in this vow? (*repent*)

Ask the confirmands to pair up, and have each person stand facing his or her partner. The pair should select one person to play the part of "sin." The other person will still be a confirmand.

Instruct the confirmands to turn away from their partners—the "sin"—so that each "sin" is facing a confirmand's back. Then have partners switch roles and repeat this activity.

Say: "This activity may seem strange, but it illustrates the meaning of the word *repent*. Repenting is more than just feeling sorry or regretting something that we've done; it also involves turning away from that behavior."

supplies
❏ *Credo Confirmation Multimedia Teaching Tools* (the DVD)
❏ equipment with which to show DVD videos

Video Option: Accept
(5–10 minutes)

If you have a copy of *Credo Confirmation Multimedia Teaching Tools*, open this session with the "Accept" video segment. This video introduces the second confirmation vow.

FREEDOM RULES!

(15 minutes)

Hand out hymnals.

Read aloud the second vow, from page 34 of *The United Methodist Hymnal,* together as a group:

> Do you accept the freedom and power God gives you to resist evil, injustice, and oppression in whatever forms they present themselves?

Say: "This vow is about the freedom that God gives us."

Ask:

> ❧ What words and images you do associate with freedom?

Record these ideas on a markerboard. When you are finished, look over the list and point out any examples that connote permissiveness or living without rules or boundaries.

Then say: "Sometimes we think of freedom as being allowed to do whatever we want. But freedom without boundaries can lead to chaos."

Challenge the confirmands to name some things that they are free to do but that they will not be able to do if they are not disciplined. (For instance, they are free to become collegiate athletes, architects, neurosurgeons, or concert musicians; but they will not achieve any of these goals unless they have extraordinary discipline.) Talk with the students about how a lack of discipline can place limits on what we can do and how it actually makes us less free.

Say: "Too often we think of discipline as something that constrains or limits us; it usually is not something that we associate with freedom. But as we've discovered, discipline is really more like training. As Christians who accept God's gift of freedom, we need to understand that the more disciplined (or well-trained) we are, the better equipped we are to do the work that God calls us to do and to live the abundant life that God desires for us."

Explain that discipline, or spiritual training, was so important to John Wesley that he created a list of rules and disciplines that he expected people in his Methodist societies to practice.

Refer back to the General Rules handouts from earlier. Set out the large paper or posterboard and assorted art supplies; and ask the youth, in pairs or trios, to make posters promoting the General Rules. Each group may create a poster publicizing all three of the rules or focusing on one of the three. Encourage creativity.

SUPPLIES

❏ copies of *The United Methodist Hymnal*
❏ copies of the "General Rules" handout
❏ markerboard
❏ marker
❏ large sheets of paper or posterboard
❏ assorted art supplies

PREPARATION: Make copies of the "General Rules" handout, from the website.

While the confirmands work, ask:

❧ How easy or difficult is it to be faithful to these three rules?
❧ What are some additional examples of doing no harm (beyond the ones Wesley has provided)?
❧ What are some additional examples of doing good?

Allow each group to present its poster. Display the posters in your meeting space or (preferably) elsewhere in the church building where others can see them.

Transformers (optional)
(10 minutes)

supplies
❑ copies of the "Transformers" handout

preparation: Make copies of the "Transformers: Christians Who Chose to Change the World" handout. Write on a markerboard the questions in the activity.

Divide the youth into groups of 2 or 3, and give each group a copy of the "Transformers: Christians Who Chose to Change the World" handout. Assign each group one of the persons profiled on the handout. Have the groups read about their assigned person and discuss the following questions, written on a markerboard:

❧ How did this person use his or her freedom to follow Christ?
❧ What forms of evil, injustice, or oppression did this person resist or reject?
❧ How do you see the power of the Holy Spirit at work in this person's life?

Give the groups 5 minutes to read and discuss, then invite the members of each group to tell the others about their assigned person and how they answered the questions.

Video option: Confess
(5–10 minutes)

supplies
❑ paper
❑ pens or pencils

preparation: Do this activity yourself. Be prepared to read to the confirmands the confession that you write.

If you have a copy of *Credo Confirmation Multimedia Teaching Tools*, open this session with the "Confess" video segment. This video introduces the third confirmation vow.

Signed, Sealed, Delivered
(10–15 minutes)

Ask a volunteer to read aloud the third vow (below and on page 34 of the hymnal):

> Do you confess Jesus Christ as your Savior,
> put your whole trust in his grace,
> and promise to serve him as your Lord,
> in union with the church which Christ has opened
>   to people of all ages, nations, and races?

Then ask:

❧ What comes to mind when you hear the word *confession*?

Say: "Often people associate the word *confession* with guilt, apology, or penitence. And honestly admitting our mistakes *is*

an act of confession. But confession is much more than just telling people that we messed up."

Hand out paper.

Say: "Imagine that you have been arrested because of your faith, and you have decided to write a full confession of your 'crime.' As clearly as possible, write what you believe to be true about your faith and your relationship with God. When you have finished, sign your name to your confession."

Read aloud your confession as an example.

Be patient with the youth during this exercise. This may well be the first effort by some of them to express their faith in words, and some of them might struggle. Some youth might not be ready to write out such a confession. Be clear that this is a "no wrong answers" activity. It is not a trap or an attempt to coax them into saying things that they do not believe or understand. The purpose of the activity is merely to help the confirmands gauge where their relationship with God stands.

Give the confirmands plenty of time to write their confessions. If some of them would like to volunteer to read aloud what they have written, invite them to do so.

Then ask:

- ❥ How difficult was it to put your beliefs into words?
- ❥ Before you did this activity, how much thought had you given to what you believe and why?
- ❥ Did you come to any new realizations about your faith while writing your confession? (Invite confirmands to explain these realizations if they feel comfortable doing so.)

TRUST: THE ONE WHO KNOWS
(10 minutes)

Once again read the third confirmation vow:

Do you confess Jesus Christ as your Savior,
put your whole trust in his grace,
and promise to serve him as your Lord,
in union with the church which Christ has opened
    to people of all ages, nations, and races?

Say: "This vow is a confession. It is also a vow of trust."

Ask:

- ❥ What does it mean to trust someone?
- ❥ How do you decide how much you will trust someone?

Ask the confirmands to spend a few moments thinking about the people they trust most. Ask a volunteer to describe whom he or she trusts most and to tell why. Were there specific actions that made a certain person trustworthy?

supplies
❏ Bibles
❏ copies of *The United Methodist Hymnal* or of the "Confirmation Vows" worksheet

preparation: Make copies of the "Confirmation Vows" handout, from the website. Think about examples from your own life about what kinds of things you would or would not trust with your most-trusted person. Make these general examples.

supplies
❏ Bibles

Then ask the youth to narrow their list of trustworthy people to a single person.

Ask:

- ❥ Who is the one person you trust more than anyone else? (The confirmands need not tell the name of the person whom they trust more than any other person.)
- ❥ Is there anything with which you would not trust the person you identified? (If the youth are reluctant to talk about what they will or will not trust this person with, spark conversation with examples from your own experience.)

Then ask a volunteer to read aloud **Proverbs 3:5-6.** Ask:

- ❥ How is putting trust in God similar to and different from trusting another person?
- ❥ How much do you trust God with the day-to-day details of your life?
- ❥ What, if anything, keeps you from fully trusting God with every aspect of your life?

CLOSING RITUAL

(5 minutes)

Gather the confirmands into a circle. During the first unit, "Know Your Story," you led this time of prayer. During the second unit, "Confirm Your Faith," one of the confirmands took the lead in closing each session. During this unit, "Live Your Commitment," no one person will lead this time of prayer. Instead, go around the circle; and allow each person to offer a prayer thanking God for your time together and all that the group has learned and experienced and asking for God's guidance as you go forth.

Close this prayer time by saying aloud and in unison the benediction, John Wesley's Rule.

NOTE: Before you dismiss, instruct the confirmands to read, reflect on, and journal about the material in the "Renounce, Reject, Repent," "Accept," and "Confess" sections of the CREDO STUDENT JOURNAL before your next session.

supplies
- ☐ markerboard
- ☐ marker

preparation: Write the benediction, "John Wesley's Rule," on a markerboard; or print out the poster from the website.

Prayers, Presence, Gifts, Service, and Witness

INTRODUCTION

Let's take a moment to look at the difference between joining The United Methodist Church and the local congregation. To the average person in the congregation, the charge to a new professing member to support the church with his or her prayers, presence, gifts, service, and witness might just sound like the next in a series of questions (to which the new member inevitably answers, "I will"). But when we look closely at the covenant in *The United Methodist Hymnal* (part of "Baptismal Covenant I," on page 38), we notice that this vow to support the church isn't just another question. It gets its own section, with a title in all capitals and everything: "RECEPTION INTO THE LOCAL CONGREGATION." Why? One answer is that this section allows a distinction between persons joining the congregation from another United Methodist congregation and those joining from another faith tradition or no faith tradition. Yet these words point to a deeper, more personal commitment; they are a call to a life of faith, of hope, and of love in a particular faith community.

Our relationship with God demands that we live in relationship with our fellow human beings. But how? What does it look like to live in relationship with others as part of a Christian community? What does God expect of us? One way to answer that question would be to say that God expects us to support the ministries of the church—and particularly those of our local congregation—through our prayers, presence, gifts, service, and witness. (Note: The 2008 General Conference added *witness* to the vows, thus it is not included in the vows as they appear in *The United Methodist Hymnal,* which was published in 1989.)

prayers

We find in the Gospel of John, in the closing chapters, Jesus saying prayers for his disciples and all to follow. And the New Testament Scriptures are replete with instructions for and examples of how to pray (see **Matthew 6:5-13** and **James 5:13-18**). By praying with and for our local congregation, we draw closer to our fellow believers and to Christ.

presence

Presence may seem like the most obvious component of church membership, but there's more to "presence" than showing up at the church building once a week. Sometimes "presence" visits people at the hospital or reaches out to someone who hasn't attended worship or Sunday school for a while. On occasion, "presence" has to restore a broken relationship. Young people who are always on the go and have several things constantly competing for their attention might struggle to be fully present in a community of faith. But if they devote themselves to setting aside time for God and for others, they will find the experience liberating. **Psalm 139** shows the enduring presence, knowledge, and depth of care that God has for us. In the story of Ruth, Scripture illustrates what human devotion to presence looks like.

GIFTS

Many of us struggle to claim the gifts that God has given us— sometimes, because we don't recognize these gifts or because we don't want to sound boastful—but the evidence of such gifts in our lives is overwhelming. There is no arrogance in realizing that we possess talents, abilities, and personality traits that can be of service to the church. Paul tells us in **1 Corinthians 12** that certain gifts are held in higher esteem than others but that each person possesses abilities that are vital to the body of Christ. Many adolescents are unaware of or are reluctant to acknowledge their own gifts. As Christian ministers to young people, we must affirm their gifts and help them find ways to return these gifts to God in the form of love—love for God, others (including enemies and strangers), and self.

SERVICE

We put our gifts to use by living a life of Christian service. We serve our congregation and, together with our congregation, we serve God's children in our community and around the world. Our service points to the example of Christ and bears testimony to God's work in our lives. Young Christians need to be made aware of the many opportunities they have to serve, whether by being an acolyte, helping an elderly member of the congregation, or being part of a Volunteers in Mission team.

WITNESS

Our witness brings together all of these expressions of faith. When we use our prayers, presence, and gifts in service of God to others, we act as witnesses to God's redeeming love through Christ and as examples of how to live a life of Christian discipleship.

As confirmands consider their confirmation vows and consider making a covenant relationship with the church, they should examine how they have supported, and will continue to support, the ministries of the church, through their prayers, presence, gifts, service, and witness.

SUPPLIES AND PREPARATION

BASIC SUPPLIES

- ❏ Bibles of various translations
- ❏ markerboard or large sheets of paper
- ❏ markers
- ❏ pens or pencils

- ❏ clear tape and/or glue
- ❏ masking tape
- ❏ index cards or paper cut about the same size (3-by-5 or 4-by-6)
- ❏ sheets of posterboard

- ❏ paper (Use paper that has already been used on one side as much as possible, depending on the activity.)
- ❏ scissors

ACTIVITY	PREPARATION	OTHER SUPPLIES
Opening Ritual	Have on hand supplies for the youth to add fruit to the vine.	❏ vine from previous sessions ❏ vine fruit (1 for each student) ❏ copies of *The United Methodist Hymnal*
A Creed Apart (Optional)	Make a copy of "Apostles' Creed" handout, from the website, for every pair of confirmands. Cut each copy of the creed into strips.	❏ "Apostles' Creed" strips ❏ optional: envelopes ❏ optional: small prize or prizes
Prayers: From the Rising of the Sun	Gather supplies.	❏ copies of *The United Methodist Hymnal*.)
Prayers: Power of Prayer	Gather supplies.	
Prayers for the Church		
Present!	Gather supplies.	❏ class roll (optional)
Presence: There for You	Gather supplies.	
Gifts: Taking Inventory	Make copies of the "Spiritual Gifts Inventory," from the website.	❏ copies of the "Spiritual Gifts Inventory"
Gifts: One to Grow on	Gather supplies.	
Service: Follow the Leader	Gather supplies.	❏ small basin of water ❏ hand towels
Service: Living It	Gather supplies.	
Can I Get a Witness?	Gather supplies.	
Closing Ritual	Write the benediction, "John Wesley's Rule," on a markerboard; or print out the poster on the website.	

OPTIONAL VIDEOS

PPGSW **Going Forth**	Preview the videos.	❏ *Credo Confirmation Multimedia Teaching Tools* (the DVD) ❏ equipment with which to show the videos

supplies

❏ vine from previous sessions
❏ vine fruit (1 for each student)
❏ copies of *The United Methodist Hymnal*

preparation: Have on hand supplies to add fruit to the vine.

note: Take time before you get started to talk with the confirmands about what they read and wrote in the "Renounce, Reject, Repent," "Accept," and "Confess" sections of their CREDO STUDENT JOURNAL.

supplies

❏ "Apostles' Creed" strips (See "Preparation," below.)
❏ tape
❏ optional: envelopes
❏ optional: small prize or prizes

preparation: Make a copy of "Apostles' Creed" handout, from the website, for every pair of confirmands. Cut each copy of the creed into strips. Keep an uncut version of the creed so that you can check the students' work.

option: Put the strips for each creed into a separate envelope to keep them together.

opening ritual
(10 minutes)

As the confirmands arrive, give each of them a cutout of a piece of fruit. Invite the confirmands to reflect on the previous session and to write on their fruit something they learned or experienced during that session. Ask the confirmands to affix their fruit to the vine. Remind them that these fruit represent ways that we, as Christians and United Methodists, live in response to God's grace.

When all of the confirmands have arrived, invite each person to talk briefly about what he or she wrote on his or her piece of fruit. (You might also ask why he or she attached the fruit to a particular branch or near a particular leaf.) Then open this session by reading aloud and in unison the "Reception Into the Local Congregation" from page 38 in *The United Methodist Hymnal*.

a creed apart (optional)
(10–15 minutes)

Before a person being confirmation vows to support the church with her or his prayers, presence, gifts, service, and witness, the entire congregation recites together the Apostles' Creed. Consider taking time in this lesson to review the Apostles' Creed, either with the activity that follows or with the "I Believe" video from *Credo Confirmation Multimedia Teaching Tools*.

Hand out a set of slips from the Apostles' Creed to each pair of confirmands. On your mark, have the pairs race to reassemble the creed. Have a hymnal (or an uncut printout of the Apostles' Creed) handy to check their work. Consider awarding a small prize to the first pair to correctly assemble the creed. Or just for fun, give a small prize to each pair as they complete the assembly.

Once all of the pairs have reassembled the creed correctly, instruct them to tape together the slips of paper, putting the tape on the back (non-printed side) of the page. (In the next activity, they'll be highlighting phrases; and most highlighter markers don't write well on clear tape.)

Then ask:

❧ How difficult was it to reassemble the Apostles' Creed?
❧ What method did you use to assemble the creed? Did you work from memory?
❧ How familiar are you with the Apostles' Creed? If you are, where and in what settings have you heard this creed?

video option: PPGSW

supplies

☐ *Credo Confirmation Multimedia Teaching Tools* (the DVD)
☐ equipment with which to show DVD videos

(5–10 minutes)

If you have a copy of *Credo Confirmation Multimedia Teaching Tools*, show the "PPGSW" video segment. This video gives an overview of what we mean by prayers, presence, gifts, service, and witness.

prayers: from the rising of the sun

supplies

☐ copies of *The United Methodist Hymnal*

(15–20 minutes)

Say: "Prayer is obviously an important part of the Christian experience."

Ask:

> ❧ What are some examples of prayers that we use in our worship services? (*a pastoral prayer, the Lord's Prayer, a prayer of confession, any liturgical prayer for special services*)

Hand out hymnals. If you have a large group or few hymnals, students may share; but make sure that everyone can see a hymnal. Instruct the students to open their hymnal to page 876, "Orders of Daily Praise and Prayer." Read aloud the opening section.

Ask:

> ❧ Did you know that there is an order of service intended for daily use by United Methodists while away from church? Have any of you ever participated in such a service?
> ❧ Why, do you think, does our hymnal include these services?

Then have the confirmands read the "Prayer of Thanksgiving" (877) from "An Order for Morning Praise and Prayer," followed by the "Prayer of Thanksgiving" from "An Order for Evening Prayer and Praise" (878).

Ask:

> ❧ What stands out to you in each prayer?
> ❧ How are these two prayers similar? different?

Ask the youth whether they have a practice of beginning and ending their day in prayer. (They need not answer aloud.) If they aren't in the habit of praying in the morning and evening, challenge them to take on this practice.

preparation: Ask a volunteer to loudly and proudly read the prepared prayer.

prayers: power of prayer

(10–15 minutes)

Have a volunteer open this activity by reading aloud the following prayer:

> O Great and Glorious Lord of Hosts and the embodiment of all that is holy, I thank thee this day for the great honor and privilege of addressing you before all these gathered here. May they be blessed as I have already been blessed in my life; may their love for you grow to be as large and sincere as my own. Be with any of them who are struggling; because, although I am not struggling myself, I can tell by the look in their eyes and also by the way some of them dress that some of them have sadness in their hearts. Thank you for loving me as much as you do so that I can sometimes, perhaps, share that love with others. Amen.

Pause to allow the confirmands to react. Then ask them to talk about their impressions of the prayer and whether the prayer seemed sincere.

Ask a youth to read aloud **Matthew 6:5-6** and **Luke 18:9-14.** Then ask:

> ❧ What do Jesus' instructions on prayer tell us about the prayer we just heard?

Ask volunteers to read aloud Jesus' prayer in **John 17,** each person reading a few verses at a time. Then ask:

> ❧ For whom is Jesus praying in this passage? (*his disciples*)
> ❧ When has someone prayed aloud for you in your presence? How did this make you feel?
> ❧ Have you ever prayed aloud for someone in his or her presence? What was that experience like?

prayers for the church

(5 minutes)

Say: "Those who are confirmed in The United Methodist Church vow to serve and support the church with their prayers."

Then ask:

> ❧ Do you think to pray for the church when you are saying prayers? Why, or why not?
> ❧ What sorts of things can and should we pray for when we pray for the church?

PRESENT!

SUPPLIES
☐ Bibles
☐ class roll (optional)

(10–15 minutes)

Take attendance. Ask the confirmands to say, "Present," when their names are called. After taking roll, ask:

➤ When you said, "Present," what did you mean?
➤ Is it possible to be in attendance without being fully present? Explain.

Select three volunteers. One will read aloud **Psalm 139:1-10**. The other two will be "present" in very different ways. One will be physically present, but will not be paying attention to the Scripture. This person can play up his or her role by rolling his or her eyes, pretending to doze off, playing on his or her phone, and so on. The final volunteer will be fully present. This person will give the Scripture his or her full attention, making eye contact with the reader and possibly even jotting down notes.

Following this demonstration, discuss the difference between how the two volunteers were present during the reading. Ask:

➤ What does it mean for us to be fully present?
➤ How can we be fully present at church, whether in worship, in Sunday school, while working on a service project, at choir practice, or while participating in another ministry of the church?

PRESENCE: THERE FOR YOU

SUPPLIES
☐ Bibles

(10–15 minutes)

Review **Psalm 139:1-10**. Ask:

➤ How aware are you of God's presence in your life?
➤ In what ways is God present with us?
➤ According to this psalm, when and where is God present?
➤ When in your life has someone "showed up" for you at a time when you really needed support?

Invite the youth to think about any friends or family members they can count on, no matter what. Then ask them to think about any times when their relationships with these persons were tested.

Ask a volunteer to read aloud **Ruth 1:1-19a** (ending with "until they came to Bethlehem"). Then ask:

➤ Are you as devoted to anyone as Ruth was to Naomi? Are you as devoted to God as Ruth was to Naomi and the God of Israel?
➤ How can you show the same level of devotion to the church—your faith family and your friends in Christ?

GIFTS: TAKING INVENTORY

(15 minutes)

Hand out copies of the "Spiritual Gifts Inventory." Ask the confirmands to complete it and identify their spiritual gifts. (If you would like or if time is a concern, you could have them complete this inventory beforehand on the website.)

Invite each person to name his or her spiritual gifts, as identified by the "Spiritual Gifts Inventory."

GIFTS: ONE TO GROW ON

(10–15 minutes)

Gather the youth into a circle. Begin by turning to the person on your left and use only one word to affirm something about that person. The affirming word should not be related to a person's appearance but to his or her positive character and personality traits. The person you affirm should offer a one-word affirmation to the person to his or her left. Continue around the circle until you receive a one-word affirmation.

Then make a list on a markerboard of all of these one-word affirmations. Ask:

❧ How did it feel to be affirmed?
❧ Were you nervous as your turn approached? Why, or why not?

Ask a youth to read aloud **1 Corinthians 12:4-7**. Then ask:

❧ Why is it so important that God gives us a variety of gifts?
❧ What, do you think, did Paul (the author of this letter) mean by "for the common good," in verse 7?
❧ How have you been able to use your gifts to serve God and others?
❧ How can you use your gifts to support the ministries of the church?

SERVICE: FOLLOW THE LEADER

(15–20 minutes)

Read aloud **John 13:3-15.** (Jesus washes his disciples' feet.)

Say: "In Jesus' day, foot washing was something that a servant did as a courtesy for a house guest. Back then, the average person's feet were almost always filthy from walking barefoot or in sandals. Foot washing was a dirty job, and it certainly wasn't something that a teacher did for his disciples."

Ask:

❧ Why, do you think, did Jesus wash his disciples' feet even though doing so was unusual and unconventional?

Say: "In remembrance of the example that Jesus set by humbly serving his disciples, we're going to wash one another's hands."

(Be clear that this exercise is symbolic. There is no need for anyone to go overboard by scrubbing another person's hands.)

Gather the youth into a circle. Dip a towel into the bowl of water, wipe the hands of the person to your right; then dry his or her hands with a second towel. This person should wipe and dry the hands of the person on his or her right. Continue around the circle until someone washes your hands.

Say: "The custom of foot washing, while common in Jesus' time, has fallen out of practice in our culture of pavement and closed-toed shoes."

Then ask:

➤ What are some similar acts of humble service that we could perform in our culture today?

➤ By washing his disciples' feet, Jesus humbly served others in his community of faith. How can you serve people in our faith community and the faith community as a whole? (This could include acolyting and participating in music ministries.)

Service: Living It
(10–15 minutes)

Supplies
❏ Bibles
❏ markerboard
❏ marker

Have a student read aloud **Isaiah 1:16-17.**

Then ask:

➤ Who are the oppressed, the orphans, and the widows in our community? (Focus on all persons who are vulnerable, not just people who are literally oppressed or are literally orphans or widows.)

Have the confirmands sit in a single-file line, one behind the other, facing you. On your mark, each person, beginning with the person at the front of the line, must call out an act of service that could be performed in your community. As soon as the first person has called out something (such as "wash people's cars") the next person takes a turn; and that person must immediately shout out another act of service. If someone fumbles and can't come up with an act of service or comes up with one that has already been said, that person must jump up and run to the back of the line. After the person at the back of the line calls out an act of service, the person at the front should call out another act of service. Continuc to a designated time or until it gets silly. Write on a markerboard the acts of service that the youth call out.

Following the game, read through the acts of service listed on the markerboard. (Feel free at this point to discard any silly ones that you may have accepted for the purpose of keeping the game going.)

Discuss each act of service, having the youth consider how your congregation is already involved in each or how the congregation might become involved in each. As a class, choose one act of service with which your church is not already involved, and develop an action plan for your group to perform this act of service.

Ask:

> ❥ What did this exercise teach you about our church's involvement in service in our community?

Then invite the confirmands to reflect on which acts of service they are involved in or have been involved in and which they could take on in the coming weeks and months.

supplies
❏ Bibles
❏ one half sheet of paper for every confirmand
❏ pens or pencils

CAN I GET A WITNESS?

(15 minutes)

The 2008 General Conference added "witness" to the list of ways in which members vow to participate in the ministries of the congregation. While printed hymnals include only "your prayers, your presence, your gifts, and your service," the vow—from the "Reception Into the Local Congregation"—should now read:

> As *members* of this congregation,
> will you faithfully participate in its ministries
>   by your prayers, your presence, your gifts,
>   your service, and your **witness**?

Ask:

> ❥ What comes to mind when you hear the word *witness*? What does it mean to be a witness?

Ask a volunteer to read aloud **John 13:34-35.**

Say: "Jesus says that people will know that we are his followers by the way we love."

Hand out half sheets of paper. Challenge each youth to list five ways in which they can show people Jesus through their love. These ways might include performing acts of service, showing love to an enemy, befriending a stranger, and so on.

Then ask a volunteer to read aloud **Romans 1:16-17.**

Ask:

> ❥ Why would someone be "ashamed" of the gospel? (Explain that *gospel* literally means the "good news" about Jesus Christ.)
> ❥ How can you proclaim the gospel without shame?

Have the youth list on the other side of their half sheets five ways that they can tell people the good news about Jesus. While telling the Good News may involve simply having a conversation with someone, it might also involve writing a song, telling their faith story online, inviting a friend to church, and so on.

Encourage the confirmands to keep their lists, perhaps in their Bible.

Say: "If you choose to take the vows of confirmation, you will promise to be a witness for Jesus whether you're at church, at home, at school, among friends, or someone else. When people know that you're a Christian, all that you do and say reflects on Christ. It's a big responsibility, but it's also a tremendous blessing."

video option: going forth
(5–10 minutes)

If you have a copy of *Credo Confirmation Multimedia Teaching Tools*, close this session with the "Going Forth" video segment. This video acts as a benediction for the entire *Credo Confirmation* program, so the Closing Ritual would not be needed.

closing ritual
(5 minutes)

Gather the confirmands into a circle. Go around the circle and allow each person to offer a prayer thanking God for your time together and all that the group has learned and experienced and asking for God's guidance as you go forth.

Close this prayer time by saying aloud and in unison the benediction, John Wesley's Rule.

supplies
❏ *Credo Confirmation Multimedia Teaching Tools* (the DVD)
❏ equipment with which to show DVD videos

note: Before you dismiss, instruct the confirmands to read, reflect on, and journal about the material in the "Prayers, Presence, Gifts, Service, and Witness" and "Going Forth" sections of the CREDO STUDENT JOURNAL.

supplies
❏ markerboard
❏ marker

preparation: Write the benediction, "John Wesley's Rule," on a markerboard; or print out the poster from the website.

CREDO Retreats Introduction

retreat to advance

Retreat in order to advance? Sounds like a contradiction. In military terms, we equate *retreat* with *defeat*. But in spiritual growth terms, we retreat to advance; we move away to draw close; we withdraw to be drawn in. Retreats help us be still in a world that is constantly "on." Rather than being a way to escape from life, retreats help us move forward in life with a deeper sense of peace, purpose, and partnership with God and others in the family of faith. Rather than being an end in themselves, retreats are an opportunity to begin again, to go back into the world and advance the cause of Christ.

Why should you do retreats as a part of the confirmation process? Retreats literally help us get away so that we can get close—close to God, close to our confirmation friends and leaders, and close to our sense of being. Retreats can be of various lengths and in a variety of locations; but they should be long enough and far enough away, either in miles or in change of surroundings, for participants to really "get away" so that they can "move toward." Retreats allow us to move

—away from distractions, such as cell phones, videogames, television—toward a focus on God's presence and movement in our lives; toward being still and knowing God.
—away from voices that constantly seek to hold our attention, define us, and shape our worldview and values—toward the voice of God discerned in prayer and worship, and as revealed in the Bible, in creation, and in the life of Jesus.
—away from familiar surroundings, patterns, routines, and habits (ways of acting and reacting) that keep us from seeing new possibilities, thinking new thoughts, and acting in new ways (Look at Kenda Dean and Ron Foster's description of rhythm breaking, *The Godbearing Life: The Art of Soul Tending for Youth Ministry,* Upper Room Books, Nashville, 1998, 117–118.)—toward the establishment of new spiritual habits, devotional practices, and ways of responding to people after the example of Christ.

expectations for retreats and confirmation

Confirmands should attend at least one retreat. Getting away from routines and familiar settings provides valuable opportunities for deep spiritual reflection and an intimate connection with God and others. Choose to lead the following retreat or prayer lock-in (see pages 101–115 and 116–122), or search one of the many United Methodist annual conferences and districts that host confirmation retreats for a retreat that your group may participate in.

MOVING TOWARD ONE ANOTHER

Retreats are great ways for young people to experience Christian community. *Community*, in this sense, goes beyond the simple designation of people who happen to live in the same town. "Christian community" is unique for several reasons. First, Jesus Christ is at the center of this community. He is the heart and soul of the group—not only of the individuals in the group. Christian community is a gift bestowed by the Holy Spirit—a gift of deep connection, relationship, shared identity, and common calling. Community is about being known and knowing others more deeply.

Common experiences of worship, devotion, and service in the name of Christ bind people together as a community of disciples. Most of the time, we gather in a Christ-centered community in weekly spurts of worship, in small groups such as Sunday school classes or youth groups, and for the occasional service project. Retreats, with their unique content, removed setting, and concentrated time frames, help us come to a deeper sense of connection, belonging, and identity as disciples of Christ in a Christian community.

RETREATING'S GREATEST HITS

Some elements are common to many spiritual-growth retreats because they get to the heart of the matter, blending content and application, experience and reflection, heart and head, intention and commitment:

- **Candles/Fire/Flame:** Candles—whether in a circle, in a procession, or on an altar—create a sense of peace, awe, and wonder and amplify our awareness of the presence of Christ among us. Bonfires provide a unique setting for worship, witness, and fellowship.
- **Circles:** Gathering into circles gives us a unique look at our faith community. As we worship, we witness to one another across and around the circle, in sharp contrast to the rows in which we often sit for worship. Circles symbolize both the eternity of God and the unity of our group in Christ.
- **Worship:** All of our retreats should include times for worship. Worship may include songs and prayers, Bible reading and reflection, witness, and prayer. Worship, in its fullness, offers something for the head (some thought or perspective that makes us think), something for the heart (some story, witness, or song that touches us in a place too deep for words), and something for the hands (something tangible that engages the senses and amplifies the message of the service).
- **Sacramentals:** Sacramentals are rituals that include prayers and symbolic elements that look and feel a lot like the sacraments of Holy Communion and baptism but are not. These can involve the use of stones, water, oil, or

any other physical elements used in rituals that convey God's grace and wisdom. Examples of sacramentals include remembrances of one's baptism (by dipping one's hand in water or pulling a stone from a basin of water), love feasts (sharing a simple meal of bread and water), and blessing participants by anointing them with oil. These kinds of rituals do not require the presence of clergy. However, if you decide to incorporate Holy Communion into one of your retreats, make sure that a clergy person is present to officiate.

❧ **Opportunities for public witness and commitment:** Young people need the opportunity to bear public witness to their faith in a safe, trustworthy, sacred space. Retreats should include a designated place or a devoted object that will help participants speak from their hearts. A designated chair, a tree stump, or a sturdy box would work. Some groups use a special walking stick, a candle, or an object that has meaning for the group, such as a shell or a handmade cross passed to each speaker, in turn. Depending on the maturity of the group, participants should be given the opportunity for deeper levels of self-disclosure, confession, repentance, and commitment. Anything from simply talking about a favorite part of the retreat to asking for prayer or expressing a new or deeper commitment to Christ should be encouraged.

CONNECTING DOTS AND CULTIVATING AH-HA MOMENTS

The CREDO confirmation sessions are divided into three units: "Know Your Story," "Confirm Your Faith," and "Live Your Commitment." The included retreat and day of prayer are designed to supplement, not to replace, the content covered in the sessions.

"Retreat to Advance" begins with group-building experiences and includes the exploration of call, identity, and ministry. The retreat could be held as a kick-off for confirmation, a mid-program burst of community, or as a closing act.

"Day of Prayer" gives confirmands a taste of several practices and experiences of prayer.

Retreats give your group the chance to live out the values of Christian community and United Methodism and help confirmands connect some dots in their understanding of what it means to be the church. Be sure to work a retreat into your confirmation schedule to give the students time away and the brain/heart space to listen for God call and to experience God's embrace.

CREDO: Retreat to Advance

INTRODUCTION

The chief task of adolescence may well be identity formation, asking and answering the question, "Who am I?" Unless they are intentional about this task, people become "whatever" people. That is, they become whatever they have been paying the most attention to—whatever has captured their imagination—often with little or no critical reflection or conscious thought.

Many voices call out to youth, inviting them, challenging them, even threatening them to believe and behave in particular ways. These voices promise acceptance, value, belonging, and success if youth listen and none of these things if they don't listen. Young adolescents are becoming more intentional about which voices they will listen to, give credence to, trust, and follow. The purpose of this retreat is to move participants toward a deeper relationship with Jesus Christ and others in the community of faith called the Church.

The confirmation journey is, in large measure, an exercise in choosing the voices we listen to. When Adam explained to God that he was hiding because he was naked, God asked, "Who told you that you were naked?" (**Genesis 3:11**). A follow-up question might be, "And why did you trust him or her?" This retreat will help confirmands sort out the voices and tune in to the voice of God as heard in Scripture; in the life and tradition of the Church; in the counsel of their trusted mentors, teachers, and role models; and in the experiences of their lives.

A well-known bank, quantum physicists, and the prophets and rabbis of the Bible all agree, "The right relationship is everything." Only in relationship do we have being and identity. Other related questions include, "Who am I in relationship with others?" and "Who am I in relationship with God?" and "Who am I in relationship with Jesus, through the Church?" and "What is my role as a Christian in this world?"

SUPPLIES

You may be able to gather many of these materials in a scavenger hunt of the church resources closet or classrooms. Ask participants whether they have any of these items. Be creative and substitute materials as needed.

- ❏ copies of the following items from the website:
  —Morning Watch 1
  —Morning Watch 2
  —Jesus and Me
  —John Wesley's Covenant Prayer
- ❏ CREDO CONFIRMATION STUDENT JOURNALS or notebooks
- ❏ recreation equipment and games for free time
- ❏ low table such as an end table or a plant stand
- ❏ large, white candle (to be the Christ candle)
- ❏ a lighter or matches
- ❏ nametags
- ❏ balloons, 9-inch rounds of assorted colors, one balloon for each person (with a few extras in case of popping)
- ❏ markerboard and/or large sheets of paper and broad-tip marker
- ❏ assorted markers, pens, and pencils
- ❏ permanent markers
- ❏ assorted fabric paints and brushes (Fabric paints in squeeze bottles are easier to use for writing on fabric, while the brush-on kind can be easier to use in large areas.)
- ❏ assorted tempera paints and brushes, fabric paint pens, fabric pencils
- ❏ long strips of fabric for stoles: medium-weight, white twill or heavy broadcloth (with sizing) cut into 5-by-52 to 5-by-60 strips (one for each participant, plus a few extras)
- ❏ sheets of construction paper, cut in half
- ❏ paper, several sheets per person
- ❏ tape, masking and transparent (no specific activity but may come in handy)
- ❏ paper lunch bags, one for each person
- ❏ index cards or slips of paper— any useful size and color— number of persons in the group times the number of persons in the group (For instance, if there are 6 members in the group, multiply 6 by 6—equals 36. If there are 10 people in the group, multiply 10 by 10— equals 100 index cards.)
- ❏ sheets of 2-by-4 labels— number of persons in the group times the number of persons in the group (The same number labels as the number of index cards, above.)
- ❏ optional: *The United Methodist Book of Worship*
- ❏ copies of *The United Methodist Hymnal*
- ❏ songbooks and/or lyric sheets (Be mindful of copyright laws.)
- ❏ musical accompaniment: guitar or other instruments
- ❏ food for all of the meals
- ❏ eating and serving utensils
- ❏ cups
- ❏ plates and bowls
- ❏ napkins
- ❏ ordained clergyperson
- ❏ Communion elements (bread and grape juice, consecrated by an elder of the church)
- ❏ chalice or other common cup
- ❏ plate for the Communion bread
- ❏ linen napkins for the Communion elements
- ❏ free-standing cross, candles, colored fabric, and other items to create the altar setting
- ❏ Communion elements and altar ware for Holy Communion

FRIDAY PM

Plan to eat along the way to the retreat site, or prepare and eat the evening meal once you arrive at your retreat site. Upon arrival, settle into your rooms. Then set up your meeting space, including a worship center or an altar table, and prepare materials for the first session.

SESSION 1: BE YOU (2 HOURS)

Group Covenant
(15 minutes)

Call everyone together, and open with prayer and a couple songs.

Review your group's covenant or any expectations for members of the retreat community. Or have the group develop a community covenant, spelling out behavioral expectations, which all members of the retreat community will sign.

Mailbags
(10 minutes)

Give each participant a paper lunch bag, and invite him or her to write his or her name on it and decorate it. These bags will become their mailbags for the weekend. Encourage the confirmands and adult volunteers to write encouraging and thoughtful messages on index cards or slips of paper and drop them into one another's bags throughout the weekend. (Pay close attention to mailbags that seem to be getting few notes, and tap some of the more mature confirmands to write notes to put in them.) Of course, all of the adult leaders will need to write to each of the confirmands.

Balloon Exercise
(15 minutes)

Give each participant a balloon. Instruct the participants to blow up their balloon and tie the end closed. Tell them to hold the balloon by the tied, knotted end. (Some participants will find it challenging to blow up the balloon and/or tie the end in a knot. Be ready to help. And some participants will find it difficult to hold their balloon still until everyone finishes.)

This activity has two "rounds," but don't let the group know that.

Round 1: Create a box on the floor using tape that is large enough so that all of the participants can stand comfortably within it. Tell the participants that when you say, "Go," they

---

Optional Supplies
- ❏ food
- ❏ eating and serving utensils
- ❏ cups
- ❏ plates
- ❏ napkins

Preparation: Plan when, where, and what the group will eat.

Supplies
- ❏ group covenant
- ❏ copies of *The United Methodist Hymnal*
- ❏ musical accompaniment
- ❏ songbooks or lyric sheets
- ❏ optional: marker and markerboard if the group will create a community covenant at the retreat site

Supplies
- ❏ paper lunch bags
- ❏ assorted markers, pens, and pencils
- ❏ index cards (See Supplies, on page 102.)

Supplies
- ❏ balloons, 9-inch rounds of assorted colors, one balloon for each person (with a few extras in case of popping)

---

are to toss their balloon into the air toward the middle of the box. Tell them that the goal of the group is to keep as many balloons in the air as possible by tapping them with their hands or head. They are not allowed to pick up balloons that hit the floor, nor are they allowed to touch balloons that go outside the box. Tell participants to be careful not to pop any balloons that fall to the floor. Instruct them that when you shout, "Stop!" they should let all of the balloons drop to the floor.

A few minutes into the game, the group will settle into a pattern; and the participants will have reached their ability to keep a certain number of balloons in the air. When the group has reached this point, shout, "Stop!" and have the participants let the balloons drop to the floor. Ask the participants to leave the balloons where they land, instead of retrieving them.

Ask:

- How might this balloon game represent the people of the church? (You might hear answers such as, "We are all different sizes," or "We have to work together to keep everyone 'up.' " that confirmands might reflect about balloons [people] who need more or less attention or care. They may notice that some people focus on only the balloons in the air, while others seem to care more about the ones that drop to the floor. Let the ideas flow for a while; and if necessary, prompt some replies.)
- How would you change the game to make it a better representation of our Christian community?

Round 2: Have participants retrieve any balloons that went out of bounds. Have everyone pick up a balloon from the floor. Make sure that every participant has a balloon for this round. Blow up new balloons to replace any that have popped.

Change the rules, according to the confirmands' ideas. For example: "In this round, the task is still to keep as many balloons in the air as you can. But this time, you are allowed to retrieve balloons from the floor or outside the box then bounce them back into the air with the others."

After a few minutes, tell the participants to stop and allow the balloons to fall to the floor as in the first round. Then ask:

- Now how might this game represent our group or how we want our group to be?

Spend some time discussing and reflecting on caring for one another, reaching out to those who go astray, and the nature of Christian community.

Be sure to keep the balloons, since they will be used again in the closing worship.

TWO-MINUTE AUTOBIOGRAPHY
(20 minutes)

Regather everyone for more community building. Invite each person to tell his or her life story in two minutes or less. Allow each person to speak when he or she is ready.

NAMES AND NICKNAMES
(15 minutes)

Invite each confirmands, and each adult who is present, to talk about the meaning or story behind his or her name.. Is he or she named for a particular person? Is there some significance behind the meaning of his or her name? Also ask each person whether he or she has a nickname. Is there a story behind his or her nickname? (Be sure to clarify that you are talking about nicknames that participants claim and are known by, not derogatory names.)

CLOSING WORSHIP: WHO AM I?
(30 minutes)

Scatter the balloons from the first activity on or around the altar table. Have the participants sit on the floor around the table. Hand out nametags and pens. Have each person write his or her name on the nametag and place the tag on the altar. Light the Christ candle.

Say something like: "We're here to build community on this confirmation journey. We're also here to get away from our day-to-day lives and listen for God's call. Sometimes in the busyness of our days we can lose the ability to hear God's voice. We can get so wrapped up in our daily events that we lose our focus on God's will for our lives. We can become so eager to be popular or be liked that we lose the identity God gave us and called 'good.' So we're here this weekend to be together, to search the Scriptures, to pray, to create, to retreat from the world so that we can advance from this place with a renewed dedication to Christ and to our walk with him.

Pray aloud: "Let's pray: Creator and ever-creating God, you dreamed us into being and called us to abundant life here on your earth. You long for us to know you and to recognize that we are always known by you. Would you send your Spirit among us this weekend as we make space to hear your voice? Would you create in us a new heart and give us fresh vision of who we are in you? Thank you for your grace, your mercy, your love. We give this time, our attention, our very lives to grow in that grace, mercy, and love this weekend. Amen."

Invite the youth to speak aloud what they hope to get out of the weekend. Encourage them to expect to meet God.

Sing some favorite songs together and then join together in the Lord's Prayer.

supplies
- ❏ low table such as an end table or a plant stand
- ❏ large, white candle (to be the Christ candle)
- ❏ Bible
- ❏ a lighter or matches
- ❏ leftover balloons from the "Balloon Exercise"
- ❏ nametags
- ❏ pens
- ❏ copies of *The United Methodist Hymnal,* songbooks, or lyric sheets
- ❏ musical accompaniment

preparation: Create a worship space by placing a low table in a spot where all of the participants can sit on the floor around it. Place the candle and the Bible in the center of the altar table.

Free Time

Let the participants know the available options for a period of free time before lights out. Some might choose time alone, while others might choose to be together.

SATURDAY AM

Morning Watch
(35 minutes)

Gather the group together before or after breakfast, and explain the purpose of Morning Watch. Morning Watch is a time for quiet reflection and solitude. Invite everyone to find a quiet place apart from the group. If a pair of friends choose to go to Morning Watch together, they should refrain from talking to each other.

Instruct the confirmands to take their Bibles, their "Morning Watch 1" worksheets, and pens or pencils with them so that they can look up the complete passages and write or draw their responses to the questions on the sheet. Give the confirmands 30 minutes to complete the exercise, then call the group together for the morning session or breakfast.

SESSION 2: BE WITH JESUS

Jesus and Me?
(50 minutes)

Sing some favorite songs together as you transition from Morning Watch to group time. Choose songs that focus on the love of Christ. Then pray, or invite a young person to lead the group in prayer.

Hand out copies of the "Jesus and Me?" worksheet, from the website. Instruct the participants to complete the column on the worksheet pertaining to their relationships with friends. Give them a few minutes to work, then invite them to talk about their answers.

Then have the participants return to the worksheet to complete the column pertaining to their relationship with Jesus. If youth have questions about how some of the situations apply to their relationship with Jesus, explain that "time alone" could be time spent in personal prayer or devotional reading; "time with others" could be time spent in worship or Christian fellowship. Again, give everyone a few minutes to work; then have the participants talk about their answers.

When they've had plenty of time to discuss, lead the group in John Wesley's Covenant Prayer (below and available on the website).

Covenant Prayer
(From John Wesley's Covenant Service, 1780)

I am no longer my own, but thine.
Put me to what thou wilt, rank me with whom thou wilt.
Put me to doing, put me to suffering.
Let me be employed by thee or laid aside for thee,
    exalted for thee or brought low for thee.
Let me be full, let me be empty.
Let me have all things, let me have nothing.
I freely and heartily yield all things to thy pleasure and disposal.
And now, O glorious and blessed God,
    Father, Son, and Holy Spirit,
        thou art mine, and I am thine.
So be it.
And the covenant which I have made on earth,
    let it be ratified in heaven.
Amen.

Call attention to the phrase "thou art mine, and I am thine." Then ask:

❧ How do you know that you are Christ's and that Christ is yours?

THEOTOKOS

(30 minutes)

Now that youth have spent some time thinking about their relationship with Jesus Christ, transition to thinking about what that means for them and how they live out their chosen-ness.

Invite a volunteer to read aloud **Isaiah 43:1-3.**

Say: "The prophet Isaiah reminds us that God claims us, saying, 'You are mine.' "

Ask:

❧ What is something that is yours that you don't want anyone else to mess with?
❧ To what lengths will you go to protect this thing?

Ask a volunteer to read aloud **John 15:16.**

Say: "Jesus said, 'You did not choose me but I chose you.' Jesus' teaching in this verse ties into baptism in our United Methodist tradition. We believe that baptism is a sacrament through which God claims us. Those who were baptized as infants were not able to choose *to be* baptized or *not to be* baptized. Baptism is also a ritual through which the church claims us. However, in confirmation, we accept for ourselves the responsibilities of being part of the body of Christ, the church."

Ask the participants whether they recall any people in Scripture whom God called for a particular purpose. As needed, introduce some of the following examples:

- Noah (**Genesis 6:11-22**)
- Moses (**Exodus 3:1-12**)
- Gideon (**Judges 6:11-24**)
- David (**1 Samuel 16:1-13**)
- Jeremiah (**Jeremiah 1:4-11**)
- The woman at the well (**John 4:1-42**)

Then review these two biblical "call" stories, and ask the related questions:

- **1 Samuel 3:1-9:** What can we know about Samuel's age in this story? What is the relationship between Eli and Samuel? How did Samuel learn to hear and respond to God's call?
- **Luke 1:26-38:** How did Mary hear God's call? How did she respond? Did Mary have a choice? What was Mary's calling?

Say: "Some Christian traditions give Mary the Greek title *Theotokos*, which means 'God-bearer'—one who brings God into the world. Mary was called to bring God into the world in a very special way, by giving birth to Jesus Christ. But all of us have a responsibility to bring God into the world."

Ask:

- How are you called to bring God into your world
- In other words, how can people around you see God in you?

JOB DESCRIPTIONS
(30 minutes)

Have the group brainstorm a list of things that would be included in the job description of a minister. What does a minister, pastor, or priest do? Record these items on a markerboard.

supplies
- Bibles
- markerboard
- marker

Ask:

> ❧ What on this list are we, as Christians, *not* called to do?

If participants question whether all Christians are called to preach, teach, or visit the sick, remind them that not all preaching comes from a pulpit in a church and that not all teaching happens in a classroom. Remind the participants that Jesus instructs us, in Scripture, to visit the sick and imprisoned. As necessary, refer to Scriptures such as **Matthew 25:31-40; 28:18-20;** and **Acts 1:8.**

Ask a volunteer to read aloud **John 14:12.** Then have the group brainstorm a list of the "works" that Jesus does. Record their responses on a markerboard.

Say: "Jesus tells us that, as his followers, we will do all of these things as well as even greater things. We are blessed to be partners in Christ's ongoing mission."

Ask a second volunteer to read aloud **1 Peter 2:9-10.** Then ask:

> ❧ Who is the "you" whom Peter refers to (as in "You are a chosen race")? (*The early Christians in Peter's original audience and us, Christ's followers today.*)

Say: "If you are a minister, raise your hand."

Tell the group that every person should raise his or her hand. Refer to the Scriptures, above, as needed.

SATURDAY AFTERNOON

LUNCH AND FREE TIME

After lunch, give the group some free time. Also set aside some time in the late afternoon for some organized recreation. Plan about an hour's worth of fast-paced cooperative, community-building games. (Since one of the objectives of this retreat is to model Christian community, select games that emphasize cooperation rather than competition.) Links to websites and books containing such games are available at the website. Remind the participants to check their mailbags.

You may choose to take a free-time break sometime during the stole-making project (below) or to lead organized group games just to break up the day.

supplies
- ❏ food for lunch
- ❏ eating and serving utensils
- ❏ cups
- ❏ plates and bowls
- ❏ napkins
- ❏ items for free time

preparation: Be sure that writing supplies are near the mailbags. Put out items for free time.

SATURDAY LATE AFTERNOON

SESSION 3: LET CHRIST GUIDE

Say: "while many people think of a minister as an ordained clergy person, everyone who takes the vows of confirmation is a minister. This afternoon we will make stoles similar to those worn by clergy persons and other church leaders. Stoles signify the yoke worn around the neck of oxen by which oxen are guided. Jesus says to us, "Take my yoke upon you" (**Matthew 11:29**); and, "My yoke is easy, and my burden is light" (**Matthew 11:30**). Wearing a stole symbolizes being tethered to Jesus and allowing Jesus to take the lead.

STOLE MAKING, ROUND 1

(30 minutes)

Give each person a long strip of fabric that will become a stole. Set out assorted permanent markers and fabric paints, but instruct the participants to leave the materials alone until you give them instructions.

Ask:

> ❥ What is a stole? (Allow confirmands an opportunity to answer the question before allowing the adults to have a chance to answer.)

Say: "In United Methodism, ordained clergy are traditionally the only ones who wear stoles in worship. But we, like many other Christians, believe that all of Christ's followers are called to be ministers--remember, we are God-bearers to the world. So each of us will make a stole to represent our call to ministry."

Instruct the participants to lay their stole fabric on the table, with both ends, side by side, nearest them and the bend (the part that will go around their neck) farther away from them. Be sure that the stoles are not twisted, that what will be the front of each stole is facing up.

Ask participants to place their left hand on the part of the stole that is closest to their left hand. (This will be on their right side when they are wearing their stole.) Confirmands will start here, working up from the bottom, following these instructions:

1. On the lower right end, one hand-width (about 4 inches) from the bottom, write the name you prefer to be called.
2. Somewhere on this same side of the stole, above your name, write three positive adjectives that describe you.
3. Also on this side of the stole, still toward the bottom, draw a symbol to represent yourself. This could be a symbol related to an activity or interest that you're passionate about or something that you're known for among your friends and family.

Give everyone plenty of time to work, then invite each person to present what he or she wrote or drew.

Supplies
- ❏ long strips of fabric for stoles (See Supplies on page 102.)
- ❏ permanent markers
- ❏ fabric paints and brushes

STOLE MAKING, ROUND 2

(30 minutes)

Supplies
- ❑ participants' stoles
- ❑ permanent markers
- ❑ fabric paints and brushes

Instruct participants to resume work on the same side of their stole (the side that will be on their right side when they are wearing the stole).

4. Ask them write and/or draw above their work from Round 1 the various roles they play in their life. Examples include, but are not limited to, the following:

- ❧ son/daughter
- ❧ musician
- ❧ caretaker of creation
- ❧ student
- ❧ gamer
- ❧ Scout
- ❧ athlete
- ❧ friend
- ❧ tutor

5. Then instruct the participants to write the word *Christian* above all of the roles they have listed. Explain that "Christian" is their name above all names, the name that defines and shapes how they live out all of the other roles that they play.

After all of the participants have had a chance to write and/or draw all of the roles they play (including Christian), ask them to take a break from working on the stole to reflect on what they have done so far. Invite them to pick one of the roles they have listed on their stole to pair it with the word *Christian*, using *Christian* as an adjective (for example: "Christian friend." Have each person name his or her word pair. It's OK to have duplicates.

Then ask:

- ❧ How does being a Christian—a disciple of Jesus—make a difference in the various roles you play?

STOLE MAKING, ROUND 3

(30 minutes)

Supplies
- ❑ Bibles
- ❑ participants' stoles
- ❑ permanent markers
- ❑ fabric paints and brushes

Ask volunteers to read aloud each of the following Scriptures about who God says we are:

- ❧ **Psalm 8**
- ❧ **Psalm 139:1-18**
- ❧ **Isaiah 43:1-3**
- ❧ **Romans 8:14-17**
- ❧ **1 Timothy 4:12**

6. Instruct the participants to move farther up the stole on the same side and to record words, phrases, and verses about who God says we are (from the Scriptures above). Examples include, but aren't limited to, the following:

- ❧ wonderfully made
- ❧ mine
- ❧ saints
- ❧ sinners

Give the participants an opportunity to talk about the words, phrases, and verses they included on their stoles.

supplies
- ❑ participants' stoles
- ❑ permanent markers
- ❑ fabric paints and brushes

STOLE MAKING, ROUND 4

(30 minutes)

During this round, confirmands will start to work on the right side (which will be the left side when being worn).

Again, instruct the participants to lay their stole fabric on the table, with both ends, side by side, nearest them and the bend (the part that will go around their neck) farther away from them. Be sure that the stoles are not twisted, that what will be the front of each stole is facing up.

7. Tell the participants to add to their stoles symbols, words, and short phrases for the three persons of the Trinity: God the Father, Jesus, and the Holy Spirit. (For example, the word *Creator* might represent God the Father, a cross might represent Christ, and a dove might represent the Holy Spirit.)
8. Invite the participants also to add other faith words and symbols that have meaning to them. Give participants an opportunity to talk about the words, phrases, and symbols they chose and why they chose them.
9. Then ask the confirmands to think of someone who has been a role model them in their walk with God—someone who has been a God-bearer for them. Instruct each person to add to his or her stole a name or symbol for a Christian role model in his or her life.

supplies
- ❑ participants' stoles
- ❑ permanent markers
- ❑ fabric paints and brushes

STOLE MAKING, ROUND 5

(30 minutes)

Invite each participant to add to what will be the left side of his or her stole (above those things that he or she added in Round 4).

10. Add the word *Theotokos,* as a reminder of our calling to bring God into the world (See "Theotokos," above.)
11. Have the participants trace one of their hands and label the thumb and finger outlines with the letters *P, P, G, S, W* (for *prayers, presence, gifts, service,* and *witness*) so that one letter is on each of the five fingers.
12. Ask the participants to add one or more of these Scripture citations:

   ❧ **1 Peter 2:9-10** ("You are a chosen race, a royal priesthood.")
   ❧ **John 14:12** ("The one who believes in me will also do the works that I do and, in fact, will do greater works than these.")
   ❧ **1 Timothy 4:12** ("Let no one despise your youth, but set the believers an example in speech and conduct, in love, in faith, in purity.")
   ❧ Additional favorite Scriptures or inspirational quotations

13. Invite the participants to sign one another's stoles in the remaining space.

EVENING MEAL

After the meal, give the group some free time if time is available. Remind the everyone to check mailbags.

SATURDAY PM

CLOSING WORSHIP AND RECEIVING OF STOLES

(30 minutes)

Gather for closing worship, and make sure that each person brings his or her stole. The youth should not put on the stoles.

Begin by having the group sing familiar songs and by offering prayers of thanksgiving for your time together and prayers of intercession for those in need.

Invite any clergy who are present to put on the stoles that signify their roles as ordained ministers.

Then invite the adult participants to come forward and to hand their stoles to a clergyperson (or to the person leading the retreat if a clergyperson is not present). The clergyperson should place the stoles around each adult's shoulders, saying these words (or something similar):

> God bless you in your ministry of confirmation
> as part of our shared ministry in the priesthood
> of all believers and the ministry of all Christians.

Encourage the confirmands to watch and pray silently as each adults receive his or her stole.

After all of the adults have received their stole, instruct them to make a circle, leaving plenty of space between themselves for confirmands to join the circle as they receive their stoles.

Invite each confirmand to hand his or her stole to one of the adults. The adults should place the stoles around the confirmands' shoulders, saying this blessing:

> God bless you in your confirmation journey
> and your unfolding ministry as part of the
> priesthood of all believers. I love you and will
> be with you every step of the way.

Adults may add blessings and comments specific to each confirmand, as appropriate.

As confirmands receive their stoles and blessings, remind them to join the circle. When everyone has joined the circle, encourage all of the participants to look around at "the church."

Then have everyone sing a song of commitment such as "I Have Decided to Follow Jesus" (2129, *The Faith We Sing*) or "A Charge to Keep I Have" (413, *The United Methodist Hymnal*).

Supplies
- food for the meal
- eating and serving utensils
- cups
- plates and bowls
- napkins

Supplies
- completed stoles
- copies of *The United Methodist Hymnal*
- songbooks or lyric sheets
- musical accompaniment

NOTE: Although we traditionally attribute this saying to John Wesley, there is no evidence that Wesley ever actually said it. Still, Wesley's Rule has been a popular saying among United Methodists for decades and serves as a great summary of how to live our lives in response to Wesley's second General Rule, "Do good."

supplies
- [ ] items for free time

supplies
- [ ] food for breakfast
- [ ] eating and serving utensils
- [ ] cups
- [ ] plates and bowls
- [ ] napkins
- [ ] Bibles
- [ ] copies of the "Morning Watch 2" worksheets
- [ ] pens or pencils

preparation: Make copies of "Morning Watch 2" worksheets, from the website.

benediction
(5 minutes)

Gather the confirmands into a circle. Go around the circle and allow each person to offer a prayer thanking God for your time together and all that the group has learned and experienced and asking for God's guidance as you go forth. Close this prayer time by saying aloud and in unison the benediction, John Wesley's Rule. (Write this benediction on a markerboard or print out the poster from the website.)

> Do all the good you can,
> By all the means you can,
> In all the ways you can,
> In all the places you can,
> At all the times you can,
> To all the people you can,
> As long as ever you can.

free time

Offer several options for a period of free time before lights out. These options could include table games, writing notes for mailbags, and preparing materials for the next day's activities and sessions.

SUNDAY AM

morning watch
(35 minutes)

Gather the group together before breakfast (or after) and hand out copies of the "Morning Watch 2" worksheet. Remind the group to take their Bibles and find a place for solitude and quiet reflection. Allow the participants 30 minutes to complete the exercise then gather for the morning session or breakfast.

affirmation posters
(20 minutes)

Give each person a sheet of labels (such as those used in computer printers) and a half-sheet of construction paper. Instruct the participants to write on a separate label an affirming message for each person in the retreat community.

When everyone is finished writing messages, instruct the participants to write their names at the top of their half-sheets of construction paper. Then have everyone pass his or her construction paper to the person to his or her right. Instruct everyone to place on the construction paper the label with the affirming message for the person whose half-sheet he or she is now holding. Then have everyone pass that paper to the person on the right. Continue until the half-sheets return to their owners. Each person's paper should include an affirming message from every person in the community. These posters will be treasured reminders of this retreat.

COMMUNION
(30 minutes)

Close this retreat with a service of Holy Communion. Use "A Service of Word and Table II" (page 12, *The United Methodist Hymnal*). Ordained clergy will need to consecrate the Communion elements. If possible, this clergy person should be present; if not, he or she can consecrate the elements beforehand. If a clergy person is unavailable, substitute a service that doesn't involve Communion, such as "The Love Feast" service (pages 581–584 of *The United Methodist Book of Worship*).

Make sure that ordained clergy is present to administer the sacrament if you have not had the Communion elements consecrated beforehand.

Begin with your group's favorite worship songs. Use **Matthew 16:13-17** ("Who do you say that I am?") as your Scripture text for worship.

After the Scripture reading, invite the group to participate in the reading. Read the Scripture once; then go around to each person and say his or her name, followed by the question, "Who do you say that he is?" If a participant feels led, he or she may speak a response such as "He is the Son of God." or "He's my savior." Or he or she may choose to speak a prayer for more belief, such as "I believe; help my unbelief."

Songs related to Holy Communion might include the following:

❧ "Time Now to Gather" (2265, *The Faith We Sing*)
❧ "Taste and See" (2267, *The Faith We Sing*)
❧ "Be Present at Our Table, Lord" (621, *The United Methodist Hymnal*)
❧ "Let Us Break Bread Together" (618, *The United Methodist Hymnal*)

Toward the end of The Great Thanksgiving, before The Lord's Prayer, invite the participants to give thanks for those who have helped them on their faith journey.

Conclude with a benediction addressed to the participants, telling them to go forth as members of Christ's holy church, loved by God, and called to do the work of God's kingdom.

supplies
❏ sheets of labels
❏ sheets of construction paper, cut in half
❏ pens

supplies
❏ Bibles
❏ ordained clergyperson (See "Preparation," below.)
❏ Communion elements and altar ware for Holy Communion
❏ chalice or other common cup
❏ plate for the Communion bread
❏ linen napkins for the Communion elements
❏ copies of *The United Methodist Hymnal*
❏ songbooks or lyric sheets
❏ musical accompaniment

preparation: An ordained clergyperson will be needed to consecrate the Communion elements. If possible, this clergyperson should be present; if not, he or she may consecrate the elements beforehand.

CREDO:
Day of Prayer

INTRODUCTION

Those who take the confirmation vows make a commitment to, among other things, uphold the church with their prayers. As members of the body of Christ, we have a responsibility to be *pray-ers*—people who pray silently and aloud, alone and with others, and with our very lives. Jesus' disciples said to him, "Teach us how to pray." So prayer must be something that we can learn to do or learn to do better. This retreat will introduce confirmands to a variety of prayer forms and will help them develop the holy habits of prayer and meditation.

You may do your Day of Prayer as a day apart—a one-day experience held within your sanctuary, at the home of a church member who has some property large enough to do some walking around, at another church nearby, or at a retreat center. Or you may choose to do a lock-in-style event that is focused on rest and prayer—sort of the opposite of what a normal youth lock-in is!

It will be important to get away from phones and the temptation to split your attention between the retreat and routine responsibilities. If you don't do a Day of Prayer, you might still choose to use some of these prayer practices in a retreat or in confirmation classes.

SUPPLIES

- Bibles
- paper
- chairs
- pens, pencils, markers, and/or crayons
- copies of "The Lord's Prayer Reverse Paraphrase" handout, from the website
- copies of *The United Methodist Hymnal*
- songbooks or lyric sheets (Be mindful of copyright laws.)
- musical accompaniment: guitar or other instruments
- stopwatch or watch that displays seconds
- worship center/altar space
- healthful snacks and drinks (preferably water) for appropriate breaks
- Optional: food for a light noon meal that might be served after "A Silent Walk" or at any time that fits within the flow of the retreat. Have on hand breakfast foods if you plan an overnight stay.

OPENING SONG

(10 minutes)

SUPPLIES
☐ copies of *The United Methodist Hymnal,* songbooks, or lyric sheets
☐ musical accompaniment: guitar or other instruments

Begin with a song about prayer. Make this song a theme song for the entire retreat. Options include:

- ✦ "Teach Me How to Pray," by Chris Hughes (more information at *credoconfirmation.com*)
- ✦ "Lord, Listen to Your Children Praying" (156, *Zion Still Sings,* and 2193, *The Faith We Sing*)
- ✦ "O Lord, Hear My Prayer" (2200, *The Faith We Sing*)
- ✦ "Take Time to Be Holy" (395, *The United Methodist Hymnal*)

Following the opening song, say: "Today we will experience and practice many kinds of prayer, including silent prayers, group prayers, and prayers that involve trying out various postures. In general, this retreat is an exercise in paying attention—paying attention to the presence of God and the movement of the Holy Spirit. Let go of any distractions, such as school or other things that are going on this weekend, and be fully present."

BREATH PRAYERS

(30–40 minutes)

SUPPLIES
☐ chairs (enough for each participant to sit in one)

Invite the participants to sit in chairs and to get in a comfortable sitting position, with both feet on the floor and their back against the back of the chair.

Say: "We're going to spend a few moments becoming aware of our breath."

Instruct the participants to close their eyes and to breathe in their regular rhythm, counting slowly to themselves as they breathe in and as they breathe out. (For example, someone might count "one, two, three" as he or she breathes in and "one, two, three, four" as he or she breathes out.)

After a few moments, ask the participants to slowly open their eyes. Ask:

- ✦ How many counts did it take you to breathe in? to breathe out?

Then say: "Now I want you to breathe on my count. You'll inhale four counts, pause, then exhale four counts."

Instruct the participants to close their eyes, take a deep cleansing breath, then exhale. Have them breathe on your count, inhaling for four counts, pausing, then exhaling for four counts. Repeat this cycle several times.

Then invite the participants to open their eyes.

Say: "Now I want you to find your own deep breathing rhythm."

Tell the participants to once again close their eyes and to pay attention to how many counts it takes for them to fully fill their lungs and how many counts it takes for them to exhale completely. Instruct participants to control their breathing so that they inhale and exhale in the same number of counts (with a pause in between).

After everyone has had time to fall into a good rhythm, gently call the participants' attention back to you. Then invite them to open their eyes.

Say: "Praying to the rhythm of your breathing is an ancient devotional practice. One common Christian breath prayer is 'Lord Jesus Christ, have mercy on me.' We can pray the first part, 'Lord Jesus Christ,' as we inhale and the second part, 'have mercy on me,' as we exhale. If you breathe deeply and slowly, with a long count, you may be able to say the entire prayer as you inhale and again as you exhale."

Ask the participants to again take a cleansing breath. Invite them to repeat this simple breath prayer—"Lord Jesus Christ, have mercy on me"—in rhythm with their breathing. After they have prayed this way for a while, gently invite their attention back to you.

Explain that they may lengthen the basic prayer for longer or deeper breathing patterns. They might choose to pray, "Lord Jesus Christ, Son of God, have mercy on me, a sinner." Or they might choose to pray a different prayer, reciting the names of the people they love and whom Jesus calls them to love. For example: "Lord Jesus, I love you. Heavenly Father, I love you. Holy Spirit, I love you. Mom and Dad, I love you. Hungry persons in my community, I love you. Persons suffering from AIDS or Malaria, I love you."

After this time of prayer, invite the participants to take the first of several prayer walks. Tell them to walk around outside (or inside if the weather is bad), saying a breath prayer. Tell participants to stay together on this walk and to remain silent. Have the participants spend about 15 minutes walking.

acts prayers
(15–20 minutes)

Call the participants back together, and have them gather into a circle. Discuss their experience with breath prayer, asking questions such as:

> ❥ What did you like most about this type of prayer?
> ❥ What was most challenging about this type of prayer?
> ❥ How did you experience God through this type of prayer?

Then say: "We're going to learn a different style of prayer called an 'ACTS prayer.' "

Explain the ACTS prayer pattern:

A—Adoration: prayers of praise and expressions of love and worship

C—Confession: owning up to what we have done or said that is against God's will for us (sins of commission) or to what we have left undone, things we could have done or ought to have done that would have been right and good and faithful (sins of omission)

T—Thanksgiving: things, persons, and experiences for which we are thankful

S—Supplication: prayers of need, especially for other people (Such prayers are also known as intercessory prayers.)

Explain that the prayers they will pray that follow the ACTS pattern will be one-word or one-short-phrase prayers. Tell everyone to bow his or her head. Then go around the circle and give each person an opportunity to offer a one-word or one-phrase prayer of adoration. Tell the participants to offer a single word or phrase describing the qualities and characteristics of God the Father, Christ, and/or the Holy Spirit. These might include *Creator, holy, wonderful, great, loving, Counselor, Comforter.*

Assure the participants that it is OK to repeat words. After going around the circle, begin again by asking everyone to offer a one-word or one-phrase prayer of confession. These might include words such as *anger, greed, laziness, disrespect, neglect.*

Go around a third time, this time having everyone offer a prayer of thanksgiving ("for food," "for family," "for the church," and so forth).

Finally, invite everyone to offer a prayer of supplication ("persons who are hungry," "cancer patients," "war," and so forth).

be still and know god
(20 minutes)

supplies
☐ stopwatch or watch that displays seconds

Take a short break, then gather everyone back together.

Say: "Learning to be still is an important skill for disciples of Christ to master. Many of us are not accustomed to being still, but stillness can be a gift. As **Psalm 46** says, 'Be still and know that I am God' (verse 10)."

Challenge the participants to be completely silent for one minute. Then experiment with silence for increasingly longer periods of time (such as 2 minutes and 5 minutes). Ask the group to be aware of the sounds they hear when everyone is silent. As you enter into longer periods of silence, invite the participants to try different prayer postures. Here are some positions to try:

- palms open in front of you, instead of hands folded
- looking up, instead of looking down
- lying on your back on the floor
- praying on your knees
- praying with your face in your hands
- praying prostrate on the floor with your arms out to your side, your body in the shape of the cross

After each period of silence, ask questions such as:

- What was challenging about remaining silent for this period of time?
- How did you experience God in the silence?
- What prayer posture did you try? What did you like or dislike about this posture?

supplies
☐ Bibles
☐ stopwatch or watch that displays seconds

a silent walk
(25–40 minutes)

Invite the participants to go on a second prayer walk. Have them walk and pray for at least 15 minutes, with the goal of praying for 30 minutes. (The dynamics of your group and the layout and location of your retreat space will play a part in determining how long the prayer walk will last.) Be clear about boundaries.

Before sending everyone off, ask volunteers to read aloud **Luke 24:13-35** (the walk to Emmaus). Talk with the group about how the two disciples were walking together when a person whom they did not recognize came to join them. Of course, the disciples would realize that the person walking alongside them was Jesus, now resurrected.

Say: "As you walk together in silence, keep your hearts open for the presence of Christ with you. Keep your eyes open for anything that reminds you of Christ or his teaching or his body, the church."

Depending on your retreat setting, you might also ask everyone to bring back from the walk an object that serves as a metaphor for God the Father, Jesus, the Holy Spirit, or the Church. Examples might include a rock (like Peter's faith, upon which Jesus built his church) or a branch (which reminds us that Jesus is the vine and we are the branches).

After the allotted time has passed, gather everyone back together and discuss the experience of silently walking and being mindful of Christ's presence.

The Lord's Prayer
(20–25 minutes)

Gather the group together in a worship space. Have the group sing one of the songs mentioned in the first activity, "Opening Song" or a musical version of The Lord's Prayer (such as 2278, in *The Faith We Sing*). Then say The Lord's Prayer together.

Hand out copies of "The Lord's Prayer Reverse Paraphrase" handout, from *credoconfirmation.com*. Explain to the participants that, for each line of The Lord's Prayer, they will write a reverse paraphrase of that line—a paraphrase that gives the line the opposite meaning. For example, "Our Father, who art in heaven, hallowed be thy name," might become, "I don't need a heavenly father, and I'm going to cuss like a sailor."

Give the participants plenty of time to work, then invite volunteers to read aloud their reverse paraphrases. Ask:

- How, do you think, did this exercise give the prayer, or certain lines, new meaning?
- How, do you think, is God like a good and loving parent?
- What, do you think, does it mean when something is "holy" or "hallowed"?
- What, do you think, does it mean for God's will to be done on earth as in heaven?
- How, do you think, can you fully depend on God to provide your daily needs?
- What does it mean to you that God, through Christ, forgives your sins?
- Why, do you think, is it important that we also forgive those who sin against us? How can God give us the strength to forgive even when doing so is difficult?
- What are some of the temptations you face? How does God help you avoid or deal with temptation?
- How does God deliver us from evil?

Invite the participants to reflect on what they need to be forgiven for and whom they need to forgive.

Then ask a volunteer to read aloud The Lord's Prayer as it appears in **Matthew 6:9-13**.

OFFERTORY Preparation, REPENTANCE, and Dedication

(40 minutes)

Tell the participants that they will have 30 minutes to prepare an offering for the closing worship service (the next activity). This preparation should be done in silence.

Say: "Your offering will fall into one of two categories. One category is a *dedication offering*. A dedication offering is a personal gift, talent, or goal that you want to give to God. As you offer it, you are dedicating it to God's glory.

"The second category is a *repentance offering*. Is there something in your life that is keeping you from loving God with all your heart, mind, soul, and strength? Has something come between you and God? Is it hurting your other relationships? A repentance offering might be an unhealthful habit, a grudge

supplies
- Bible
- lyric sheets
- copies of *The United Methodist Hymnal*, songbooks, or lyric sheets
- musical accompaniment: guitar or other instruments
- copies of "The Lord's Prayer Reverse Paraphrase" handout, from the website
- pens or pencils

preparation: Make copies of "The Lord's Prayer: Reverse Paraphrase" handout, from the website.

SUPPLIES
❑ Bibles
❑ paper
❑ pens, pencils, markers, and/or crayons

NOTE: Do not expect or encourage confirmands to leave items behind, but if some decide that what they have offered has become a distraction and has kept them from focusing on their relationships with God and others, allow them to leave the item in your care. Give the item to the confirmands' parents along with an explanation of why it was left behind.

SUPPLIES
❑ worship center/altar space
❑ Bible
❑ lyric sheets
❑ musical accompaniment
❑ dedication and repentance offerings

PREPARATION:
Assemble the worship center/altar space.

that you hold, or something you have become obsessed with. As you offer it, you are asking God to help you turn away from it and turn back toward God."

Tell the participants that they should be prepared to bring some tangible representation of the offering. Dedications might include, for example, a cell phone (if excessive texting or gossiping is keeping them from God), a guitar pick (if music is one of their gifts), a piece of jewelry or an electronic device (if they feel as though they obsess too much about material things), a poem (if writing is one of their gifts). Point out that paper and writing utensils are available if they need them. Some participants may ask whether they will get their offerings back. The answer is yes, unless they choose to leave them behind. (See the note in the margin.)

Tell the participants that you will invite them to bring their offerings to the altar table. They will have the opportunity, but are not required, to tell the group about what they are bringing and why.

CLOSING WORSHIP
(20 minutes)

Gather the group into a circle for a round of prayers. One person (you as a leader or one of the other participants) will start by offering a spoken prayer about whatever is in his or her heart. When the first person finishes, he or she will gently squeeze the hand of the person on his or her right. This person then will offer a spoken prayer. Continue around the circle. If a participant is not comfortable praying aloud, he or she may simply squeeze the hand of the person on his or her right.

After this time of prayer, have the group sing some familiar worship songs, including songs about prayer (see "Opening Song," page 117). If you have chosen a theme song for this retreat, include that song as well. As the participants sing, invite them to get into prayer postures that are helpful to them.

Following the singing, invite participants to bring their dedication and repentance offerings to the altar table. Allow each person to talk about his or her offering and why he or she brought it. Take time to pray (silently and/or aloud) for each person who comes.

Finally, with hands stretched out over the offering table, offer closing prayers of thanksgiving, hope, and dedication.

Offer a benediction, and invite the participants to retrieve their offerings (if they choose to; see the margin note above) and to exchange signs of God's love and peace.

Mentoring and Confirmation

One of the primary goals of any confirmation program is to equip and inspire young people to devote themselves to lives of Christian discipleship. We do this by telling the story of our faith, introducing young people to essential Christian beliefs and practices, inviting young people to enter into a covenant relationship with the church, and making clear what will be expected of them as professing members of The United Methodist Church. But one of the most effective ways to prepare confirmands for a life of discipleship is to foster relationships between the confirmands and adults in the church who are striving to be faithful disciples.

In recent decades, many congregations have made mentoring part of their confirmation program. Generally, program leaders pair each confirmand with an adult from the congregation who is not his or her parent or close relative; or they assign one or more adults to a small group of confirmands. While mentors certainly provide leadership, they usually are not part of the leadership team in charge of teaching confirmation classes or leading retreats. Rather, they lead by walking alongside youth, offering emotional support, being present with the youth during confirmation classes and retreats, and being available to discuss with youth tough questions about faith.

EXPECTATIONS FOR MENTORING RELATIONSHIPS

Confirmands should meet regularly with a mentor. You can find information on recruiting and training mentors in this section of this resource. Be sure to adhere to your congregation or annual conference's Safe Sanctuaries standards where mentoring relationships are concerned. Also consider having confirmands and their mentors sit together in worship at least once each month.

WHOM SHOULD WE RECRUIT AS MENTORS?

Mentors should be persons with a mature faith. This does not mean that they have to be perfect Christians or that they cannot have doubts. It also doesn't mean that they have to be biblical scholars, trained theologians, or pastoral counselors. It does mean that they are committed to growing in faith, are striving to be holy, and can be honest and open about their faith.

Mentors need to love and care for the youth with whom they work, but they need to relate as adults to these youth. Some adults who work with youth fall into the trap of trying to act like youth. But no adult should see ministry with young people as an opportunity to relive his or her teenage years. As John Gooch writes in *Claiming the Name: A Theological and Practical Overview of Confirmation,* "Youth don't need more 'pals.' They need someone who is willing to relate to them as an adult."

Your congregation may already have mentors in place. Many congregations pair children with faith friends when they begin kindergarten or first grade. If children have continued these relationships, it makes sense for faith friends to become confirmation mentors. Ideally, these relationships can continue throughout the adolescent years. John Gooch suggests that every young person should have godparents who are members of the congregation. Traditionally, godparents make a commitment, upon a child's baptism, to nurture that child in faith. In cases where parents name as godparents friends or relatives who live in another state or attend another congregation, Gooch suggests that each young person have a second pair of godparents who are part of the congregation. He says that, if we really take seriously the Baptismal Covenant, it makes sense to have godparents serve as mentors for young people from baptism, through confirmation and adolescence, and into adulthood.

Karen Kluever, a youth pastor and confirmation leader at Woodland United Methodist Church in Rock Hill, South Carolina, pairs each of her confirmands with a "grandfriend," an older adult mentor/Christian friend. Some people feel as though ministry to young people is the domain of twenty- and thirty-somethings. Involving older adults affirms for an older generation that the spiritual formation of youth is a multigenerational endeavor.

Some congregations pair a single confirmand and a single mentor, while others assign one mentor to two or three youth or a pair of mentors to a small group of confirmands. Some confirmands prefer a one-on-one relationship with a mentor and are more willing to open up and discuss tough questions when peers are not present. Others prefer having the support of a group of peers with a common mentor (or mentors). All of these arrangements are acceptable if done correctly. Prayerfully consider which arrangement would best facilitate the spiritual growth of and would most honor the spiritual gifts of your confirmands and mentors.

You can find additional information on mentoring models at www.credoconfirmation.com.

Having youth meet with a single adult mentor raises safety concerns. While you should have complete confidence in the mentors you recruit and have faith that they would not harm a youth with whom they have a mentoring relationship, *Safe Sanctuaries for Youth* (a resource produced by the General Board of Discipleship of The United Methodist Church) warns, "Abusers thrive on secrecy, isolation, and their ability to manipulate their victims." It adds, "When abusers know that they will never have a chance to be alone with potential victims, they quickly lose interest in working with youth" (page 38).

To ensure that an adult mentor will never be alone with youth, require mentors to meet with youth in public places, such as restaurants or in an open space in the church. Also do not allow mentors to drive youth anywhere unless there is another adult in the car. Similar principles apply to mentor-youth conversions by phone, text-message, social-networking sites, and e-mail. Having two adults work as a mentoring team greatly reduces the risk of abuse, especially if those adults are not related. Regardless of your mentoring arrangements, you should screen potential adult mentors by doing a criminal background check. This may seem extreme, but it is one of the most effective ways to prevent abuse. (For more information on safety see the *Credo Confirmation Guide for Parents, Mentors, and Other Adult Leaders* or visit the *Safe Sanctuaries* website at www.gbod.org/safesanctuaries.)

Older youth who have been already confirmed also may play a mentoring role. Younger youth benefit greatly from relationships with older adolescents who have continued to grow in faith in the few years since they took their confirmation vows. These former confirmands set a positive example of how to stay faithful to one's relationship with Christ and the church during the teenage years; they also act as a reminder that confirmation is not an end unto itself but is one important step along one's faith journey. Many confirmation programs have involved older youth with great success. (Michael Ratliff, Associate General Secretary of the Division on Ministries With Young People, when he was in local church ministry, referred to his older youth confirmation helpers as "ex-cons.") But older teens should act as mentors in addition to, not in place of, adult mentors.

WHAT SHOULD MENTORS DO?

Simply put, mentors should walk with confirmands on the confirmation journey. Mentors should be visibly present during the confirmation experience, should be familiar with what the confirmands are learning and experiencing, and should stand with confirmands during the rite of confirmation.

Mentors should also be part of the confirmation leadership team, and they should be clear about what is expected of them. You might ask that they attend all of the confirmation class sessions or that they participate in a confirmation retreat. You might ask that they meet weekly or bi-weekly with their confirmand(s) or that they sit with their confirmand(s) each Sunday in worship. Expectations of mentors will vary from congregation to congregation, but it is essential that these expectations are clear and that mentors are thoroughly involved in the confirmation experience.

Mentors need to know that they are not teachers. They likely will learn as much from the youth as the youth learn from them. Instead of imparting knowledge, mentors should show support, invite questions, and be available to listen. They should take seriously all of the doubts, concerns, and struggles of the young person(s) with whom they are in relationship. Mentors should be honest about their faith, without passing judgment; they should be loving, without excusing bad behavior. Most important, they should set for confirmands an example of Christian discipleship.

More information on the role of mentors is available in the *Credo Confirmation Guide for Parents, Mentors, and Adult Leaders.*

HOW DO WE TRAIN MENTORS?

The first step in training mentors is to help them understand the importance of the ministry they are involved in. Confirmation is the affirmation of the faith into which a person was baptized and is a crucial step along a young person's spiritual journey. Agreeing to serve as a confirmation mentor is not a responsibility that one should take lightly.

Gather your mentors and introduce them to the confirmation program. Give each of them a copy of the *Credo Confirmation Guide for Parents, Mentors, and Adult Leaders.* Discuss with them the theology behind confirmation and the place of confirmation in The United Methodist Church. Go over the various components of the CREDO program, and take the mentors through the scope and sequence of the confirmation class sessions found in the book's introduction and on the website. Explain to the mentors their role in the confirmation experience and the expectations that you (and the confirmands and parents) have for them. Address risk management issues, and go over your congregation and/or youth ministry's safety policies. Incorporate a time of worship and devotion into this gathering, praying with mentors and allowing them time to reflect on this ministry to which they have been called. Consider providing dinner for this gathering, and be sure to provide childcare.

Develop a confirmation covenant for the mentors to sign that again explains their role and the expectations you have for them and that also lists dos and don'ts related to safety and boundaries (such as, "If you meet one-on-one with a confirmand, be sure that you are in a public place"). A sample covenant for mentors is available at *www.credoconfirmation.com*.

Throughout the confirmation experience, check in with mentors to see how they are doing, to answer any questions they may have (whether about their role or about theology or Scripture), and to see how you and other adult leaders can help them. Always make sure that mentors know that they are valued and important and that you support them in their ministry.

resources for mentors

Each mentor should have a copy of the *Credo Confirmation Guide for Parents Mentors, and Adult Leaders* (ISBN: 9781426706271). This book helps mentors understand their role, provides valuable information about adolescent faith development, and gives summaries and discussion questions for each confirmation class session.

The adult leader website at *www.credoconfirmation.com* has additional resources for mentors.

Christian Education and Confirmation

By Tim Gossett

A comic strip years ago poked fun at the state of Christian education in the life of the church; and sadly, the state is little changed. In the first panel, the pastor stands before the congregation, facing a group of about a dozen young youth and saying to the worshipers, "This morning, we recognize our confirmands...." In the second panel, which flashes forward to a similar scene a few years later, the pastor says, "This morning, we recognize our graduates...." Finally, in the third panel, the pastor looks down and sees before him only two youth, neither of whom he recognizes any longer.

The comic strip's point is unfortunately true of many congregations. Following confirmation, many youth seem to disappear from the life of the church. Perhaps the promises youth make at confirmation are empty ones, as if they had their fingers crossed behind their backs as they took their confirmation vows. But more likely, families, congregations, and the youth themselves misunderstood the purpose of confirmation and its place in the Christian life. Simply put, confirmation is not the end of the faith formation journey but just one stepping stone along a lifelong path. When he or she is confirmed, a young person should be confirming a faith that has been nurtured over time and that will continue to be nurtured throughout that young person's life.

expectations for christian education

Confirmands should participate in a Christian education setting in addition to confirmation class. This might not be possible if your confirmation classes meet during the Sunday school hour and your congregation has no other education opportunities for confirmation-age youth. (If this is the case, you might consider launching a mid-week small-group ministry.) If your confirmation classes meet on Sunday afternoon or evening or during the week (and if your congregation offers Sunday school classes for confirmation-age youth), confirmands should get in the habit of attending Sunday school each week. Consider requiring confirmands to attend Sunday school at least three Sundays per month, possibly with the option of substituting a mid-week Bible study.

CONFIRMATION AND OTHER YOUTH EDUCATION MINISTRIES

Take some time to map out all of the ways that the youth in your confirmation program are involved in the life of the church, and, particularly, in education ministries (Sunday school, youth fellowship, Bible studies, camps, vacation Bible school, and so forth). List everything you can think of, from the obvious ongoing activities to less obvious ones, such as helping in the nursery, taking a leadership role in the Easter sunrise service, or going on a church-sponsored trip to an amusement park.

If you gave this exercise careful consideration, you probably became aware that your congregation ministers to confirmation-age youth in several ways, even if your church doesn't have a formal youth ministry. All of the adults in the congregation are involved in educating confirmation-age youth, even if they are unaware of the roles that they play. Here are some ways that you can help the congregation understand these roles:

- ❧ Introduce the confirmands to the congregation toward the beginning of the confirmation process.
- ❧ Add the members of the confirmation class to the prayer lists in your church bulletin or newsletter and/or on the church website.
- ❧ Remind your congregation's ministry teams to create youth-friendly events as they do their planning.
- ❧ Occasionally mention in a sermon the confirmation mentors and the roles they play.
- ❧ Encourage members of the congregation to learn the names of the youth and children sitting near them during worship.
- ❧ Post in your church building promotional materials related to confirmation and other youth events.
- ❧ Make sure that the adult leaders involved more directly in educating the youth in your church—Sunday school teachers, youth fellowship volunteers, Bible study leaders, youth choir directors, and so on—are communicating with one another. These adult leaders need to be supportive of one another's ministries and should discuss information such as what they're studying or discussing with the youth, important dates, and concerns about the youth.

Christian Education Doesn't Start and End with Confirmation

Education is an essential part of any confirmation program. Confirmands should learn the story of their faith, as told in Scripture and in the history and tradition of the church; they should learn the core doctrines of Christianity and of The United Methodist Church; and they should learn spiritual practices and what it means to live a life of Christian discipleship. But it is unfair to expect young people to learn during confirmation classes everything they need to know about the Bible, the Christian faith, and Christian living. Christian education is a lifetime endeavor, and confirmation is an opportunity to help confirmands develop lifelong learning habits.

One way to help confirmands make a long-term commitment to Christian education is to encourage or require participation in other education ministries as well. If your confirmation class sessions meet during the evening or on Sunday afternoon, you could require or expect the confirmands regularly attend Sunday school. (You would need to make exceptions or provide alternatives for confirmands who split time between their divorced parents.) If your confirmation class sessions meet during the Sunday school hour, you might require participation in youth fellowship or a midweek Bible study.

Regardless of your arrangement, it is important that your congregation see confirmation as part of its larger Christian education ministry. Those involved in planning and teaching children's Sunday school classes should consider how they are preparing children for confirmation. Youth ministers, youth Sunday school teachers, and adult volunteers in youth ministry should build on what youth learned in confirmation and should seek opportunities to make connections between what youth are learning in Sunday school or youth group and what they learned during confirmation. Even adult Sunday school classes and Bible studies can revisit the confirmation vows. The church can provide confirmation opportunities for adults as well. After all, there is not designated age for confirmation; and in the United Methodist tradition, confirmation is a repeatable rite.

DEVELOPMENTAL CHARACTERISTICS OF YOUTH

While confirmation may seem to be a unique learning experience that is separate from other formational experiences for youth, it is not. Confirmation leaders, like Sunday school teachers and youth fellowship leaders, benefit from a familiarity with sound educational principles and adolescent development.

Your approach to teaching confirmation should be developed with attention to the characteristics of the group you are teaching. Younger youth (early adolescents) and older youth (middle adolescents) are at different stages of cognitive, physical, and social development. You'll have the best learning environment possible if you tailor your teaching to the needs of your group members. Take a few minutes to reflect on the chart on page 130, noting your own thoughts and observations about the implications of each row for your setting.

Role of a Confirmation Leader

In many congregations, confirmation falls outside of the youth and children's ministry departments. Thus some confirmation leaders—including confirmation mentors—have little engagement with other youth or children's ministries. Training adults involved in confirmation to be ministers and educators of young people is essential to a successful confirmation program. Here are a few things for confirmation leaders to know and discuss:

Leaders do not need to be experts in the Bible nor live a saint-like life, but they should have a passion for growing in their faith and in their knowledge of Scripture. It's entirely OK for a leader to say in response to a question about the Bible, "I don't know the answer to that question. Let's find the answer together." The youth should see in the faith lives of confirmation leaders evidence that they have matured beyond their own confirmation experience have committed themselves to continual spiritual growth.

Great confirmation leaders are great listeners. They pay attention to what confirmands are actually saying (verbally and nonverbally) and aren't inwardly focused on what their next question will be. They understand that they do not have to fill up silence by restating a question or providing the answer but, instead, are willing to wait patiently for youth to think about their answers to questions.

Leaders maintain appropriate boundaries with youth. This includes following appropriate Safe Sanctuaries policies adopted by the congregation, such as never meeting one-on-one with a youth or child in a room without a window or behind a closed door, having a background check done on all adult workers with children and youth, making sure that at least two adults (unrelated to each other) are always present during classes or events, and not driving with only one youth in the car. It also means being sensitive to the emotional boundaries of youth during conversations.

Leaders are not youth with a few extra years, inches, and pounds added on. In other words, adults should not try to be cool or to act like teens in order to try to gain acceptance by youth. Adults should act like adults. That *does not* mean that adults cannot have and display a youthful spirit, a joyous and fun-loving personality, an enjoyment of the things youth like, or a great sense of humor. Instead, it's a recognition that they have accepted a leadership role and will make decisions that keep the youth's best interests at heart.

Developmental Characteristics of Youth

YOUNGER YOUTH (12-14)	OLDER YOUTH (15-17)
Vary widely in growth patterns and sexual maturity, both between and within gender groups	Less range of differences in size and physical maturation
Rapid physical growth means appearance and coordination changes; are easily embarrassed by their bodies	Body image and appeal is of significant concern; eating disorders can develop
Are concerned with justice (fairness) and equality; are beginning to think abstractly, but still think largely in concrete, literal, either-or terms.	Have a greater ability than younger youth to understand moral and ethical complexity; think abstractly
Understand cause and effect, and are growing in their ability to use logic to solve problems	Like to demonstrate their acquired knowledge
Can imagine consequences for their actions	Can see issues from multiple perspectives
Desire to visit places beyond their own community	Desire to understand and visit other countries
Have a greater attention span than they did as children and are ready for in-depth, long-term engaging experiences	Generally have longer attention spans than younger youth, but lose patience quickly with activities they deem pointless
Are developing an interest in the opposite sex and want to engage with and understand each other	Seek emotional and physical intimacy with others
Their peers are their second family, and they greatly desire peer approval	Peers are still important, but service to others, beyond their peer group, is also valued
Are beginning to question authority and family or church values	See adults—including adults in positions of authority—as fallible, yet desire their respect
Prefer coming up with their own ideas and solutions to going along with ready-made ones	Wish to take on leadership roles
Are the center of their own universe	Less self-centered than younger youth; try on multiple roles and ways of being in the world
Strive for independence yet understand they need the help of adults	Are identifying their unique gifts and searching for possible vocations
Desire privacy from parents and other adults	More freely reveal their thoughts and feelings to adults than do younger youth
Are frequently forgetful and prone to making poor decisions	Can be responsible with money, jobs, and so on; but judgment and decision-making skills vary greatly among older youth
Often feel all-knowing, invulnerable, and powerful	Understand better than younger youth the fragility of all life

Credo Confirmation Teaching Plans for 8 Weeks

Leaders need to communicate with the parents or guardians of the youth—not just with the youth themselves. For example, leaders should always copy the parents when sending e-mail or text messages to set up times and places to meet. Information about schedule additions or changes should be sent to the parents and not simply mentioned to the youth.

ASPECTS OF FAITH DEVELOPMENT

Just as one passes through various phases of physical development, one also passes through different phases of faith development. But there is one significant difference between the two: Whereas physical development largely (but not entirely) is the result of genetics and age and tends to occur at a similar rate in most people, spiritual development depends on God's grace—and how one responds to God's grace—and is different for every person. One can get stuck in a particular phase of faith development or can even revert to a previous stage.

Those who study spiritual growth have described the stages of faith development in different ways. Perhaps the best-known way of identifying faith stages comes from James Fowler, in his book *Stages of Faith: The Psychology of Human Development and the Quest for Meaning*. Another important assessment of phases of spiritual maturity comes from John Westerhoff's *Will Our Children Have Faith?* Both Fowler and Westerhoff offer descriptions of faith development that are very useful in understanding the way one's faith changes over time, but Westerhoff's model is simpler and better suited for CREDO. He describes four primary stages of faith development:

1. **Experienced Faith** is common during the younger years of childhood and mainly involves the imitation of actions. For example, a child may pray the Lord's Prayer without grasping the full meaning of all of the words. Because young children are dependent on their families, there is a sense of faith identity that forms related to the family.

2. **Affiliative Faith** is common in older childhood and the early adolescent years. Here the dominant characteristic is belonging to a group, and behavior centers around imitation of the group. The individual identifies with a faith community where he or she feels a sense of belonging and in which his or her beliefs and actions are rooted. You may find that many confirmands—especially at the start of the confirmation journey—display characteristics of affiliative faith.

3. **Searching Faith** becomes more common in late adolescence and is connected with the formation of identity. A youth begins an internal and external dialogue, asking, "Is this what I believe? Why, or why not?" Youth or adults at this stage do not blindly accept what others have said to them, because they need to find certainty for themselves. This stage of faith adds a cognitive dimension to a person's faith journey, and a person going through the stage of Searching Faith begins to integrate head and heart.

Because Searching Faith is a common faith stage for confirmands, it is important to understand more about it. This questioning stage generally goes one of two ways. Some persons question the tenets of faith, the validity of the Bible, the teachings of the church, or the differences between denominations and faith systems; and they decide they can no longer believe. Youth who make such a decision might drop out of confirmation. Some youth will remain at this stage, becoming adults with an immature faith. Some become vulnerable to cults or decide that they wish to become part of another church group (especially if their friends attend elsewhere). But many—especially those who have a companion on the journey—will successfully grow through this stage and will move on to the final stage.

4. **Owned Faith,** as Westerhoff defines it, is rare until early adulthood. It can come about only as a result of growing through Searching Faith. After wrestling with the question, "Is this what I believe?" one can resolve that question for oneself. Owned faith is a strong, vital faith that one lives by, expresses to others, and would even be willing to die for. Growing into this stage of faith does not mean that one stops having or asking questions but, instead, that one has learned to embrace questions as a means to further and deepen one's spiritual connection with God and others.

CONFIRMATION AND FAMILY LIFE

Youth spend far more time with parents than with confirmation leaders and other adults they know through church. Parents and guardians have a greater influence on the lives of confirmands than the confirmation experience does. Since parents and guardians vary widely in their commitment to the Christian faith, you have no guarantee that additional faith formation happens within the home.

On the bright side, the fact that a parent requires, allows, and/or supports his or her teenager's involvement in confirmation can be his or her entry point into greater participation in the life of the church. Even if parents are not involved in the life of the congregation or have not matured in their faith, the confirmation experience of their adolescent children can spark dialogue within the family about matters of faith. Confirmation also is a time when parents tend to be more open than usual to the church's guidance when it comes to nurturing their children's faith.

Keys to Increase Parent Involvement in Confirmation

❧ Give parents faith formation resources: devotional guides, family talk sheets, and so forth.
❧ Encourage families to do a family service project—on their own or with other families—during the confirmation process.
❧ Offer a parallel confirmation class for the confirmands' parents and guardians.
❧ Let parents know that at any time they may visit with you about the confirmation program and their teen's experience.
❧ Encourage parents to pray for their confirmand and the confirmation class as a whole, and give parents an example of how to do this.

CHRISTIAN EDUCATION AND CONFIRMATION

While confirmands learn a great deal in confirmation classes, on confirmation retreats, and through other aspects of your confirmation program, they should emerge from confirmation with the understanding that Confirmation Sunday is not a graduation from Christian education. Christian education is important to a life of Christian discipleship. It provides opportunities for acquiring knowledge, questioning and articulating one's beliefs, and fellowship with Christian friends.

Congregations and confirmation leaders must create a culture in which Christian education is a practice that spans a lifetime. They can do this by making available Sunday school classes and/or other educational opportunities by people of all ages, by giving young children a solid biblical foundation so that they are prepared for confirmation as youth, and by helping youth and adults retain and build on what they learned and experienced in confirmation.

Worship and Confirmation

By Taylor Burton-Edwards
Director of Worship Resources
The General Board of Discipleship

Your confirmands likely have thoughts and feelings about worship, whether they grew up worshiping in your congregation, have recently come to your congregation after worshiping elsewhere, or are new to the church altogether. Some who have spent a week at church camp, who attend parochial schools, or who have had the opportunity to worship with several congregations have experienced worship in a wide variety of styles and settings.

One can hope that your confirmands can identify worship experiences or parts of your congregation's worship services that they enjoy and in which they have found a meaningful connection with God. Chances are, some youth will have no problem naming aspects of worship that they find boring or annoying. Maybe the music feels outdated, the prayers don't connect with them, the sermons don't answer the question they've been asking, or the Scripture readings seem either mumbled or overdone. Maybe the youth don't care for the music of the choir or the praise band, or they get frustrated by the lag between when the PowerPoint® slides are supposed to appear and when they actually do.

There are a lot of ways worship can miss its marks. And when worship misses those marks enough, it's easy to tune out or not attend worship at all. But that would be to presume that the point of Christian worship is satisfying the individual worshiper. It's not. It's about God and what God is doing with and through all of us, especially those who—as confirmands—are saying yes in answer to the yes that God said to them in the covenant of baptism.

It is possible that worship hasn't clicked for some of your confirmands because it has felt to them like a series of seemingly irrelevant, disconnected, or even

Expectations for Worship

Confirmands should attend worship each week. Weekly worship is the most comprehensive way in which a congregation rehearses its faith and is recharged by God. Those wishing to take the confirmation vows and enter into a covenant with the body of Christ and with your congregation need to attend worship for most, if not all, of the Sundays for the duration of the confirmation program. While it is best for the confirmands to worship with the congregation in which they are being confirmed, it is more important that they develop weekly worship habits. If a confirmand splits time between two parents who attend two different churches, it is OK if he or she worships with one congregation one week and with another congregation the next. It also is OK for confirmands who are spending a weekend at the home of a friend or out-of-town family member to attend worship with their hosts. Consider requiring confirmands to attend worship at least three Sundays per month (allow for exceptions in the case of family emergencies).

random acts of introspection and group excitement. But there is a deep logic that underlies the basic pattern of Christian worship and informs everything we do there. We see this logic at work in the baptismal covenant that is the basis of our confirmation vows.

THE BAPTISMAL COVENANT AND THE BASIC PATTERN OF CHRISTIAN WORSHIP

The basic pattern of our Christian worship, from the earliest days, can be described as a drama in four acts. In Act I, Entrance, we gather from many places and assemble ourselves as the body of Christ to offer ourselves in praise and thanksgiving to God.

In Act II, Proclamation and Response, we hear Scripture read and proclaimed; and we respond with affirmations of faith and prayers for the church and the world.

In Act III, Thanksgiving and Communion, we present ourselves to God as a living sacrifice, with gifts of bread and cup, and receive them back again as body and blood of Christ.

And in Act IV, Sending Forth, we are sent into the world to live more faithfully as disciples of Jesus. (See *The United Methodist Hymnal*, page 2.)

If that pattern is practiced well, the flow of one act into another comes to "feel right" over time. But we don't worship just to keep the flow going. We don't even worship for the sake of the drama as a whole. Rather, we worship because we know that, through the drama and each of its four acts, we are participating in a living, active reminder of God's yes and our desire to keep saying yes. In other words, through Christian worship, we rehearse God's covenant with us in baptism and find ourselves recharged to live more faithfully into this covenant.

The Entrance act of worship is more than just a beginning, a gathering, or a time to settle down and reconnect with God. It is for us, as it had been in early Christianity, an assembly around the baptismal font. Many United Methodist (and other Christian) congregations have restored the ancient practice of placing the baptismal font near the entrance of the worship space so that persons can see and touch the water and remember their baptism as they enter. Even if the font is not or cannot be placed near the entrance of the worship space, a greeting or some opening words spoken around or near the font reminds us who we are and who we are called to become.

Confirmands, who are considering and/or preparing to say yes to God's yes, need to understand that we become members of Christ's body, the church, upon baptism. Confirmation is a means of affirming and professing our membership.

The Proclamation and Response act is an assembly around the Word of God revealed in Scripture and preaching. This is why, in many churches, worshipers stand for the reading of the Gospel text and/or other Scriptures. In Christian worship, we read Scripture—not just as good advice for our lives but because we believe that Scripture contains "all things necessary to salvation" (Article V of The Articles of Religion of the Methodist Church). Salvation is not simply insurance for the life to come, but is participation and partnership in all the ways that God works to transform the world and deliver God's creation from captivity to sin and death. Those who say yes to God's yes seek guidance, correction, and support from Scripture and the proclamation of the gospel so that we may "work out [our] own salvation" (**Philippians 2:12**) and live more faithfully into the covenant we've made with God and the church.

Thanksgiving and Communion is an assembly around the Lord's Table. When we pray for the Holy Spirit to be poured out on us and on the gifts of the bread and the cup that we offer, we are asking not only to be in communion with Christ but also that in receiving his body and blood "we may be for the world the body of Christ redeemed by his blood" (*The United Methodist Hymnal*, page 10). Confirmands need to understand that Holy Communion is more than just a "holy moment." Holy Communion is a reaffirmation of our pledge to take Christ into the world, which we do in worship's final act, Sending Forth.

But the relationship between Christian worship and saying yes to God's yes goes even deeper. The vows that we say yes to are remembered and rehearsed in Sunday worship.

THE CONTENT OF THE COVENANT IN CHRISTIAN WORSHIP

❖ **Do you renounce the spiritual forces of wickedness, reject the evil powers of this world and repent of your sin?**

This vow is, in effect, an act of treason against every authority on earth, except that of God in Jesus Christ. Renunciation is an active and intentional breaking of allegiance. Rejection means not recognizing the claim of another to have authority over you. Repentance means changing one's whole mindset, one's whole consciousness. The question about repentance isn't simply about feeling sorry for specific things we have done or left undone. Repentance means that we turn and pledge to keep turning away from all we had thought or done that sprang from any allegiance to evil or any claim it made or may ever again try to make on our lives.

When we gather around the font and remember our baptism during the Entrance, the first act of worship, we also remember where our allegiances lie and that we are offered the "mind of Christ" (**1 Corinthians 2:16; Philippians 2:5**) instead of the "wisdom of the world" (**1 Corinthians 1:18-25**). When we assemble around the font, whether literally or imaginatively, we continually remind ourselves that we have renounced and will continue to renounce, reject, and repent of any allegiance, claim or action that does not align with the way of Jesus, our one Lord. For "there is one body and one Spirit, just as you were called to one hope of your calling, one Lord, one faith, one baptism" (**Ephesians 4:4-5**).

❖ **Do you accept the freedom and power God gives you to resist evil, injustice and oppression in whatever forms they present themselves?**

It is one thing to renounce evil; it is quite another to stand against a dismantle evil wherever it appears. When we say yes to God's yes, we pulled into the struggle against evil. This is why worship includes Scripture reading and preaching. Scripture and preaching are the n explicit ways in worship that we are made more aware of our faith limitations in resisting evil, reminded to re-claim our strengths and gifts, and empowered to exercise the freedom and power God gives us to better resist evil in the days ahead.

❧ Do you confess Jesus Christ as your Savior, put your whole trust in his grace, and promise to serve him as your Lord, in union with the church which Christ has opened to people of all ages, nations and races?

The confessions "Jesus Christ is Lord" and "Jesus Christ is Savior" were also acts of treason during the first several centuries of Christian history within the Roman Empire. The titles "Lord" and "Savior" belonged specifically to the Emperor and to no one else. By using such names for Christ, the early Christians not only negated the claim that Caesar was Lord or Savior, but they also redefined the terms *lord* and *savior*. While affirming that Christ rules over all, Christians understand Christ's rule to be the rule of God's kingdom and of love and justice.

At its most basic, Christian worship rehearses us in the first three parts of this vow. We confess that Jesus is Lord and Savior and "put our whole trust in his grace" throughout every "act" of Christian worship—in greetings, songs, hymns, the reading of Scripture, sermons, confessions of faith and sin, acts of pardon, prayers, sacraments (both baptism and Holy Communion), benedictions, and sending forth.

But Christian worship also should rehearse us in the last part of the vow. When we gather as congregations on Sunday morning, we do not (and must not!) gather as separate "generational" or "ethnic" or "cultural" groups. Doing so would violate our baptismal covenant. This does not mean that such groups may not gather for all sorts of purposes, also involving worship, at other times and places. But for Sunday worship, we are called to gather together across generations, across ethnic and cultural lines, and across the many other barriers that divide us. By gathering in such a way, we bear witness to our intention to live our lives in the world "in union with the whole church which Christ has opened to people of all ages, nations and races."

❧ According to the grace given you, will you remain faithful members of Christ's holy church and serve as Christ's representatives in the world?

In worship, we remember that God has claimed us in baptism. We listen to Scripture and preaching to better learn how to be faithful members of Christ's holy church. We confess our faith, pray for the church and the world, confess our sins, receive God's pardon, and offer one another the peace of Christ as those who have desire to grow in faithfulness. We gather around the Lord's Table to offer our gifts and ourselves as a living sacrifice to God.

All of this prepares us for the final act, the Sending Forth, where we affirm our call to "serve as Christ's representatives in the world." In the prayer of thanksgiving following Holy Communion, we ask God to "send us now into the world in the strength of your Spirit to give ourselves to others" (*The United Methodist Hymnal,* page 11). And in the dismissal and sending, we are sent forth specifically in the name and as representatives of our Triune God, blessed and reminded of God's presence with us as we go.

SUNDAY WORSHIP AS NECESSARY BUT INSUFFICIENT

Confirmands need to understand that worship is necessary and completely relevant to who we are as Christians. Sunday worship is the most comprehensive way in which a congregation rehearses its faith and is recharged by God.

Sunday worship is a necessary part of Christian discipleship. But it is not sufficient. Nor is it meant to be. Sunday worship summarizes and deeply expresses our call to discipleship, but it does not substitute for our living out that call in our daily lives. To do that, we must do what Jesus himself told his disciples: "If any want to become my followers, let them deny themselves and take up their cross daily and follow me" (**Luke 9:23**). This means that worship is not just something we do with the congregation on Sunday. Worship is something we do every day, albeit in ways that are different than the ways we worship on Sunday. Connecting with God through daily prayer, Scripture reading, devotional reading, and conversation with Christian friends also are important ways that we worship.

Introduce confirmands to some of the resources that are available for daily worship and reflection, including "An Order for Morning Praise and Prayer" and "An Order for Evening Praise and Prayer," in *The United Methodist Hymnal* (pages 876 and 878, respectively) and *Devo'Zine,* the daily devotional magazine for youth published by The Upper Room. Additional daily worship resources are available at *www.credoconfirmation.com.*

But confirmands also need to understand that worship is not the only thing we do as Christians. The baptismal covenant should influence all aspects of our lives, and it helps to have a small group of Christian friends who meet regularly and hold one another accountable to the vows they have taken. Covenant Discipleship groups, which confirmands learn about in the "Way of Discipleship" session, are one way in which United Methodists have come together in small groups to offer one another support and accountability.

Confirmands, who are considering saying yes to God's yes, should be expected to worship with the congregation every Sunday. (Although we must also understand that, due to illness or divided families, this is not always possible.) They also should get in the habit of worshiping throughout the week though prayer, reflection, and Scripture reading. Such practices of worship should become for them what God intends them to be—a means of grace by which the Holy Spirit works to transform them more and more fully into the image of Christ.

CONFIRMATION SUNDAY WORSHIP SERVICE

The entire congregation needs to understand how important confirmation is to the life of the church. The confirmation Sunday worship service is an opportunity to lift up the ministry of confirmation while also creating a memorable experience for those being confirmed. Young people celebrate all sorts of milestones—earning the Eagle Scout rank or Girl Scout Gold Award, being inducted into National Honor Society, winning an athletic competition, or graduating from high school—with memorable ceremonies and rituals. The rite of confirmation should be at least as meaningful and memorable as these other important adolescent moments. The confirmation Sunday worship service should make clear the importance of confirmation in the life of the congregation and of those being confirmed.

Here are some things to keep in mind as you plan your confirmation Sunday worship service:

❧ **Confirm during your regular Sunday worship service.**
Confirmation, by its nature, involves the entire community of faith. Thus it is important that the whole congregation participate. Sunday afternoon or weeknight confirmation services for parents and families cut out the rest of the congregation and deny church members the opportunity to vow to "nurture one another in the Christian faith and life and include [those being confirmed] in [their] care" (*The United Methodist Hymnal,* page 35). Problems can arise if a congregation has two or more Sunday worship services. If this is the case in your congregation, consider confirming at all of these services or confirming at one service but recognizing the confirmands and the entire confirmation ministry at all services.

❧ **Include the entire Baptismal Covenant I in your confirmation service.**
The Book of Discipline says, "Becoming a professing member requires the answer of faith of the baptized person made visible in a service of profession of Christian faith and confirmation using the vows of the Baptismal Covenant." The vows of confirmation listed in the *Discipline* are the basis of Baptismal Covenant I (which begins on page 33 of *The United Methodist Hymnal*) and of the sessions in the "Live Your Commitment" unit of this confirmation program. Thus all of the vows in the Baptismal Covenant I service are essential to the rite of confirmation and the responsibilities of a professing member of The United Methodist Church.

The rest of the service also is essential. The "Thanksgiving Over the Water" puts the covenant of baptism in the context of our faith story (from the waters of creation to Jesus' command to baptize and make disciples of all nations), invokes the Holy Spirit, and reminds us that confirmation is an act of God's grace for which we should be thankful. The reciting of the Apostle's Creed allows the congregation to affirm the faith of the church into which the confirmands are being confirmed.

❧ **Include in the service parents, mentors, and other members of the congregation involved in confirmation.**
While the pastor has the responsibility of organizing confirmation classes and while the youth minister, the children's minister, and/or a dedicated volunteer may act as a confirmation teacher or director, an effective confirmation program requires the time and effort of many church members, including parents, mentors, siblings and other family members, Sunday school teachers, retreat leaders, children's or youth choir directors, and so on. All of these people can participate in the confirmation rite by standing with the confirmands and by laying hands on persons being confirmed. You might also invite mentors to say some words on behalf of the confirmands they've worked with, letting the congregation know how these young people have grown in faith through the confirmation process.

❧ **Incorporate your vine and stoles into the service.**
The opening ritual for the confirmation class sessions involves creating a vine, or tree, inspired by **John 15:1-9.** At the beginning of each session,

Credo Confirmation Teaching Plans for 8 Weeks

confirmands will add branches, leaves, or fruit to this vine. There are several ways that you can create this vine: Your group could paint a vine as a mural on the wall of your meeting space; you could draw or paint a vine on a large sheet of paper, posterboard, or butcher paper; or you could build a three-dimensional tree using wood, dowel rods, and craft materials. If your tree or vine can be moved into your worship space, have it on display during the confirmation worship service. Consider reading aloud some of the words and phrases that the confirmands wrote on the branches, leaves, and fruit.

As part of "Retreat to Advance," each of the confirmands creates a stole to represent their call to be a Christian disciple and a minister of the gospel. Place a stole around each confirmand's neck as he or she is confirmed.

SUGGESTED HYMNS FOR CONFIRMATION SERVICE

From *The United Methodist Hymnal:*
- On Eagle's Wings (143)
- Seek Ye First (405)
- The Church's One Foundation (545 and 546)
- We Are the Church (558)
- Pass It On (572)
- This Little Light of Mine (585)
- Here I Am, Lord (593)

From *The Faith We Sing:*
- I Have Decided to Follow Jesus (2129)
- Cry of My Heart (2165)

From *Zion Still Sings:*
- Thy Way, O Lord (159)
- I'm Determined (175)

From *Worship & Song:*
- Covenant Prayer (3115)
- How Shall I Come Before My Lord? (3124)

Mission and Service and Confirmation

By Lanecia Rouse

"Teacher, which commandment in the law is the greatest?" He said to him, " 'You shall love the Lord your God with all your heart, and with all your soul, and with all your mind.' This is the greatest and first commandment. And a second is like it: 'You shall love your neighbor as yourself.' On these two commandments hang all the law and the prophets."

—Matthew 22:36-40 (NRSV)

Do all the good you can,
By all the means you can,
In all the ways you can,
In all the places you can,
At all the times you can,
To all he people you can,
As long as ever you can.

—commonly attributed
to John Wesley

OUR HERITAGE: A PEOPLE CALLED [UNITED] METHODIST

EXPECTATIONS FOR SERVICE

Confirmands should fulfill a service requirement. Service should be completed through the ministries of the congregation and may include participating in traditional service projects, helping with ministries to homeless and/or hungry persons, assisting with vacation Bible school, or serving as an acolyte or other worship leader. Require each confirmand to complete five or six service hours during the course of your confirmation program.

Throughout our history, we United Methodists—and those of our predecessor denominations—have understood ourselves as a people called to love God with our whole hearts, souls, and minds and to love our neighbor as we love ourselves, in response to the two greatest commandments (**Matthew 22:34-40**). Participating in God's work of healing, hope, and radical love is essential to being faithful to these commandments and is a central part of the United Methodist tradition.

While John Wesley affirmed that salvation comes entirely through God's grace, he often preached about the importance of means of grace, practices through which we more fully experience God's grace. These means of grace include praying, reading Scripture, and taking Holy Communion; but they also include doing acts of mercy and justice.

Wesley, as well as other leaders throughout our United Methodist history, taught that we Christians should live our lives with regard for the humanity and well-being of all persons.

Mission and Service: A Way of Life

Throughout Scripture, we encounter stories of people whom God calls to offer hope to the hopeless, freedom for those who are oppressed, sight to those who are blind, food for the hungry, water for those who thirst, comfort for those who mourn, shelter for the homeless, and clothing for those who are naked. Jesus began his earthly ministry by reading from the **Book of Isaiah:** "The Spirit of the Lord is upon me, because he has anointed me to bring good news to the poor. He has sent me to proclaim release to the captives and recovery of sight to the blind, to let the oppressed go free, to proclaim the year of the Lord's favor" (**Luke 4:18-19**). Later Jesus teaches that when we feed the hungry, give water to the thirsty, clothe the naked, take care of the sick, and visit the imprisoned, we are feeding, clothing, caring for, and visiting Jesus himself (**Matthew 25:31-40**).

Serving others in a spirit of Christ's love is essential to living a life of Christian discipleship. In and through mission and service, young people bear witness to Christ's presence, offer their gifts to join in doing the work of God's kingdom, and learn to love while also receiving love. Confirmation is a great opportunity to help young people better understand Christ's call to live missional lives. As we are called to participate in this particular stage of their faith journey, we have a responsibility to prayerfully discern ways for confirmands to offer their gifts in love of and service to their neighbors—both inside and outside the church. God uses mission and service experiences to do incredible things through the lives of those who are offering themselves in service and those who are receiving the gift of embodied love. (And often in these experiences, the lines between giver and recipient quickly become blurred.)

Serving: Being Present

Helping young people claim their identities as children of God and disciples of Christ is central to the confirmation process. And engaging the youth in mission and service opportunities is crucial to teaching young people what it means to be Christian disciples. Few confirmands have the opportunity to embark on a missional journey to Haiti or Burkina Faso to work alongside people who are suffering from poverty or malnutrition or dehydration. But they nonetheless can participate in meaningful mission and service experiences that will draw them closer to God and neighbor. Whether these experiences involve singing or playing music at a local retirement home, serving warm meals to persons without a home, or helping lead vacation Bible school programs for younger children, the experiences should help young people:

—understand the importance of community and our need to be in relationship with other persons;
—discover new passions and callings or affirm existing passions and callings;
—form relationships with persons from various walks of life;
—strengthen relationships with persons they know who are joining them in service;
—encounter Christ in new ways as they seek to be the presence of Christ to others;
—be agents of change as they step out in faith with God; and
—love others as Christ first loved us.

Mission and service experiences allow young people to participate in the healing and restoration of those who are wounded, suffering, and broken; understand the Gospel in new ways; and experience everyday resurrections. The confirmation journey is an ideal time for young people to connect with God and their neighbors through mission and service.

Service-Learning: Reflection and Growth

While it is great for young people to get their hands dirty in service to others, confirmands are most likely to make mission and service a way of life if they have an opportunity to reflect on the work they have done. What did they learn about the need they sought to address? What did they learn about the people they served and worked with? How did they serve Jesus by reaching out to persons in need (**Matthew 25:31-40**)? How did they experience God's kingdom on earth (**Luke 17:20-21**)?

Service-learning adds another dimension to service by giving those who serve an opportunity to reflect on their service experience. While service involves meeting a need, service-learning also involves understanding the need and considering its sources. While service is an act of giving to those whom we serve, service-learning is also an act of receiving from those we serve. While service is about doing something for others, service-learning also is about being in relationship with others. As you engage your confirmands in mission and service, make sure that they have time to reflect on their work before, after, and during the project. Challenge them not only to help persons in need but to strive to understand and be in relationship with persons in need. And help confirmands understand service as an act of faith and a way of showing our love for both God and neighbor.

Discernment: Being Open

Because mission and service experiences are so important to the spiritual formation of young people, those of us who connect confirmands to these experiences have a responsibility to practice prayerful discernment when choosing and/or creating mission and service opportunities. Raking leaves on a Saturday in the fall or working at a soup kitchen once a year are not the only ways that young people can be in mission. When we take time to be in prayer about how God is calling us to join in loving and serving the world, we often find the Spirit taking us to places we might not ordinarily go to be with people we otherwise might not choose to be with. And we might find that these experiences require more than a few hours each year.

As you discern, consider and pray about the following questions:

- How is God calling your confirmands, at this time in their life, to give and receive God's love?
- What gifts do your confirmands have to offer, either as individuals or as a group?
- What are some of the needs of your local, national, and global community?
- Specifically, who, within a five-mile radius of your church building, needs to experience Christ's transforming love?
- How might God use your confirmands' gifts to respond to some of the needs you have identified? How can you confirmands be instruments of God's love to persons who need to experience this love?

In response to **Matthew 25:31-40,** say a prayer asking Christ to show you where he is hungry, naked, orphaned, lonely, thirsty, imprisoned, sick, or oppressed and to point you to ways that your group can provide Jesus with food, clothing, family, community, water, health, or freedom.

You may discover that God is calling your group to offer a creativity camp for children in your neighborhood who are eager to offer something beautiful to the world. You may discover that God is calling your confirmands to serve meals to a group of homeless persons once a month, joining in table fellowship with strangers, and developing relationships over time. You may discover that your confirmands' gifts and passions are suited for eradicating hunger or ending child slavery by standing up to the forces that perpetuate these injustices. The young people in your confirmation group could then become teachers and agents of change in your community. Who knows what opportunities God may be creating or leading you toward? As you prayerfully ask and pray about these questions, prepare to be divinely surprised.

As you discern, learn about and be aware of ways in which people are already working to meet the needs you have identified. People and organizations who are already actively responding to these needs have valuable knowledge and experience and likely have already worked through the logistical challenges of starting a mission and service ministry. Instead of starting from scratch, look for ways to assist and partner with these groups. While joining those who are already in the field is a good tactic for anyone involved in mission or service, it is very important for those who identify as United Methodist Christians. The United Methodist Church is a connectional church. Within the connection, countless congregations, annual conferences, boards and agencies, and church-sponsored organizations are hard at work healing a variety of wounds in their communities and throughout the world. Each of these efforts is an opportunity to strengthen the connection by bringing more people together around a common calling and purpose.

LOGISTICS: BEING PREPARED

An important part of preparing mission and service experiences, is making sure that you have adult leaders in place who can care for and support the young people as they serve. As you use discernment to select mission and service opportunities for your confirmands, also use discernment in selecting adult leaders. Do not simply enlist anyone who is available; but seek adults who have gifts, passions, and knowledge that will help the young people learn and grow from the mission or service experience. We have a responsibility to do all that we can to create an environment where confirmands can encounter "the abiding love of God and fellowship within the community of faith" (*Safe Sanctuaries for Youth*, page 8).

The United Methodist Church encourages all congregations to have a Safe Sanctuaries policy in place to reduce the risk of abuse of the young people whom God has called us to love. If you partner with organizations that provide mission and service opportunities for youth, make sure that these organizations have similar policies and protections in place.

As the first Christians went out into the world, they usually had a friend by their side. When working with young people, it is best to have by your side a friend who can see what you might not see, hear what you might not hear, and hold you accountable to the goals and expectations you have for your ministry.

It is also important to invite the parents of your confirmands and other members of the congregation to join the group in mission or service. Make sure that you meet with parents at least once in advance of any mission or service project. Provide parents with logistical information (where you will serve; why you have chosen to serve in this particular way; what the confirmands will be doing; what safety precautions you have taken; costs and fundraising strategies; food, lodging, and transportation details; and all of the calendar dates related to the project).

Give the parents any permission slips, medical release forms, and/or insurance and health forms; and let parents know of ways that they can be in prayer for the group. Parents are entrusting their children to your care. One of the responsibilities that goes along with this privilege is making sure that parents have the information they need to support and share in the mission or service experience.

Like the confirmands' parents, the congregation also has entrusted to you the lives of the young people of the church. Therefore, you also have a responsibility to let the congregation know what the confirmands are doing and how members of the church may support their young people in mission and service. Keep the congregation informed by making announcements during worship and by posting updates on the church's website, blog, or social-networking webpage.

Enlist members of the congregation to be prayer partners for each person (confirmand and adult leader) who is participating. Before the mission or service project, prepare (with the confirmands' help) a short presentation to let Sunday school classes and small groups know what the confirmands will be doing. Following the projects, have the confirmands prepare a short presentation for these classes and groups, telling about what they did and learned from their mission or service experience. Young people are eager to be creative; and many are gifted in using various forms of media to tell their story. In addition, their presentation will be a blessing to the congregation.

DISCIPLESHIP: TAKING GOD'S LOVE INTO THE WORLD

As disciples of Christ, regardless of our age, we are called to love and serve God and neighbor. Every day, we have opportunities to offer God's transforming and redeeming love to those who are desperately in need of being loved. Confirmands need to understand that mission and service are essential to who we are as followers of Christ. May you discover great joy and grace as you empower, equip, and encourage your confirmands to live a life of mission and service grounded in the life, ministry, and resurrection of Christ.